Stephen Greenblatt is a leading figure of new historicism and one of the most influential writers on Shakespeare and early modern culture. Questioning not just literary but social, political and cultural assumptions about knowledge and power, Greenblatt's work has had a huge impact on contemporary theory.

Mark Robson outlines the central features of Greenblatt's work, examining:

- exactly what new historicism means and the relevance of new historicism to all aspects of literary criticism
- the development of Greenblatt's work on crucial topics such as self-fashioning, social energy, resonance and wonder, and imagination
- the style of new historicism, including features such as the anecdote, story-telling and the essay
- the relationship of Greenblatt's work to romanticism, formalism and historicism, culture, ghosts, theatre and religion.

Offering a starting point for readers new to this crucial theorist's texts, or support for those deepening their understanding of his work, this guidebook is ideal for students in the fields of literary studies, history, social and cultural studies.

Mark Robson is Lecturer in English at the University of Nottingham. He is author of *The Sense of Early Modern Writing* (2006), co-author of *Language in Theory* (2005) and editor of *Jacques Rancière: Aesthetics, Politics, Philosophy* (2005).

ROUTLEDGE CRITICAL THINKERS

Series Editor: Robert Eaglestone, Royal Holloway, University of London

Routledge Critical Thinkers is a series of accessible introductions to key figures in contemporary critical thought.

With a unique focus on historical and intellectual contexts, the volumes in this series examine important theorists':

- significance
- motivation
- key ideas and their sources
- impact on other thinkers

Concluding with extensively annotated guides to further reading, *Routledge Critical Thinkers* are the student's passport to today's most exciting critical thought.

Already available:

For further details on this series, see www.routledge.com/literature/series.asp

STEPHEN
GREENBLATT

Mark Robson

Routledge
Taylor & Francis Group

LONDON AND NEW YORK

First published 2008
by Routledge
2 Park Square, Milton Park, Abingdon, Oxon OX14 4RN

Simultaneously published in the USA and Canada
by Routledge
270 Madison Avenue, New York, NY 10016

Routledge is an imprint of the Taylor & Francis Group, an informa business

© Mark Robson, 2008

Typeset in Perpetua by
Florence Production Ltd, Stoodleigh, Devon
Printed and bound in Great Britain by
TJ International Ltd, Padstow, Cornwall

British Library Cataloguing in Publication Data
A catalogue record for this book is available from the
British Library

Library of Congress Cataloging in Publication Data
Robson, Mark, 1968–
   Stephen Greenblatt/Mark Robson.
      p. cm. – (Routledge critical thinkers)
   Includes bibliographical references and index.
   1. Greenblatt, Stephen, 1943 – Criticism and interpretation.
   2. New historicism.   I. Title.
   PN75.G74R63 2007
   801'.95092 – dc22   2007011779

ISBN10: 0–415–34384–4 (hbk)
ISBN10: 0–415–34385–2 (pbk)
ISBN10: 0–203–40801–2 (ebk)

ISBN13: 978–0–415–34384–8 (hbk)
ISBN13: 978–0–415–34385–5 (pbk)
ISBN13: 978–0–203–40801–8 (ebk)

CONTENTS

SERIES EDITOR'S PREFACE

The books in this series offer introductions to major critical thinkers who have influenced literary studies and the humanities. The *Routledge Critical Thinkers* series provides the books you can turn to first when a new name or concept appears in your studies.

Each book will equip you to approach these thinkers' original texts by explaining their key ideas, putting them into context and, perhaps most importantly, showing you why they are considered to be significant. The emphasis is on concise, clearly written guides that do not presuppose a specialist knowledge. Although the focus is on particular figures, the series stresses that no critical thinker ever existed in a vacuum but, instead, emerged from a broader intellectual, cultural and social history. Finally, these books will act as a bridge between you and their original texts: not replacing them but, rather, complementing what they wrote. In some cases, volumes consider small clusters of thinkers working in the same area, developing similar ideas or influencing each other.

These books are necessary for a number of reasons. In his 1997 autobiography, *Not Entitled*, the literary critic Frank Kermode wrote of a time in the 1960s:

> On beautiful summer lawns, young people lay together all night, recovering from their daytime exertions and listening to a troupe of Balinese musicians. Under their blankets or their sleeping bags, they would chat drowsily about

the gurus of the time ... What they repeated was largely hearsay; hence my lunchtime suggestion, quite impromptu, for a series of short, very cheap books offering authoritative but intelligible introductions to such figures.

There is still a need for 'authoritative and intelligible introductions', but this series reflects a different world from the 1960s. New thinkers have emerged and the reputations of others have risen and fallen, as new research has developed. New methodologies and challenging ideas have spread through the arts and humanities. The study of literature is no longer – if it ever was – simply the study and evaluation of poems, novels, and plays. It is also the study of the ideas, issues, and difficulties which arise in any literary text and in its interpretation. Other arts and humanities subjects have changed in analogous ways.

With these changes, new problems have emerged. The ideas and issues behind these radical changes in the humanities are often presented without reference to wider contexts or as theories that you can simply 'add on' to the texts you read. Certainly, there's nothing wrong with picking out selected ideas or using what comes to hand – indeed, some thinkers have argued that this is, in fact, all we can do. However, it is sometimes forgotten that each new idea comes from the pattern and development of somebody's thought and it is important to study the range and context of their ideas. Against theories 'floating in space', the *Routledge Critical Thinkers* series places key thinkers and their ideas firmly back in their contexts.

More than this, these books reflect the need to go back to the thinkers' own texts and ideas. Every interpretation of an idea, even the most seemingly innocent one, offers its own 'spin', implicitly or explicitly. To read only books on a thinker, rather than texts by that thinker, is to deny yourself a chance of making up your own mind. Sometimes what makes a significant figure's work hard to approach is not so much its style or content as the feeling of not knowing where to start. The purpose of these books is to give you a 'way in' by offering an accessible overview of these thinkers' ideas and works and by guiding your further reading, starting with each thinker's own texts. To use a metaphor from the philosopher Ludwig Wittgenstein (1889–1951), these books are ladders, to be thrown away after you have climbed to the next level. Not only, then, do they equip you to approach new ideas, but also they empower you, by leading you back to a theorist's own texts and encouraging you to develop your own informed opinions.

Finally, these books are necessary because, just as intellectual needs have changed, the education systems around the world – the contexts in which introductory books are usually read – have changed radically, too. What was suitable for the minority higher education system of the 1960s is not suitable for the larger, wider, more diverse, high technology education systems of the twenty-first century. These changes call not just for new, up-to-date introductions but new methods of presentation. The presentational aspects of *Routledge Critical Thinkers* have been developed with today's students in mind.

Each book in the series has a similar structure. They begin with a section offering an overview of the life and ideas of the featured thinkers and explaining why they are important. The central section of the books discusses the thinkers' key ideas, their context, evolution and reception: with the books that deal with more than one thinker, they also explain and explore the influence of each on each. The volumes conclude with a survey of the impact of the thinker or thinkers, outlining how their ideas have been taken up and developed by others. In addition, there is a detailed final section suggesting and describing books for further reading. This is not a 'tacked-on' section but an integral part of each volume. In the first part of this section you will find brief descriptions of the key works by the featured thinkers; then, following this, information on the most useful critical works and, in some cases, on relevant websites. This section will guide you in your reading, enabling you to follow your interests and develop your own projects. Throughout each book, references are given in what is known as the Harvard system (the author and the date of a work cited are given in the text and you can look up the full details in the bibliography at the back). This offers a lot of information in very little space. The books also explain technical terms and use boxes to describe events or ideas in more detail, away from the main emphasis of the discussion. Boxes are also used at times to highlight definitions of terms frequently used or coined by a thinker. In this way, the boxes serve as a kind of glossary, easily identified when flicking through the book.

The thinkers in the series are 'critical' for three reasons. First, they are examined in the light of subjects that involve criticism: principally, literary studies or English and cultural studies, but also other disciplines that rely on the criticism of books, ideas, theories and unquestioned assumptions. Second, they are critical because studying their work will provide you with a 'tool kit' for your own informed critical reading and thought, which will make you critical. Third, these thinkers are critical because they are crucially important: they deal with ideas and questions that can overturn conventional understandings of the world, of texts, of everything we take for granted, leaving us with a deeper understanding of what we already knew and with new ideas.

No introduction can tell you everything. However, by offering a way into critical thinking, this series hopes to begin to engage you in an activity which is productive, constructive, and potentially life-changing.

ACKNOWLEDGEMENTS

Bob Eaglestone, Liz Thompson and Polly Dodson at Routledge provided just the right mix of encouragement and advice during the writing of this book. Lisa Freinkel's generous reading of the proposal shaped much of what I went on to write. Colleagues and students in the School of English Studies at the University of Nottingham provided much support, especially Peter Howarth, with whom I had many fruitful discussions, and Julie Sanders, who read the whole manuscript with her customary care and generosity. Special thanks must go to Elodie and to the Laügt households in Antibes and Bordeaux, whose hospitality allowed me the space to write much of the first draft. Stephen Greenblatt also deserves my warm thanks, not least for his good humour when I informed him that I was writing this book. One of the great advantages of having finished it is that I can now look forward to Professor Greenblatt's next book without the sense of dread that he might finish his before I had finished mine.

WHY GREENBLATT?

Stephen J. Greenblatt (1943–) is one of the most important literary and cultural critics working today. He is best known for his influential writings on Shakespeare and English Renaissance literature, but his work also encompasses interests in art, architecture, ritual, religion and culture in the widest imaginable sense. In a series of groundbreaking books, he has elaborated what he calls cultural poetics, a practice that has for nearly thirty years more usually been called new historicism.

As the title new historicism suggests, the central issue in Greenblatt's work has always been the relationship between works of art and literature and their various histories and contexts. His primary focus has been on early modern culture, and on canonical writers such as Christopher Marlowe (1564–93), Walter Raleigh (1554–1618), Philip Sidney (1554–86), Thomas Wyatt (1503–42), Edmund Spenser (1552?–99) and, especially, William Shakespeare (1564–1616). But one of the most intriguing things about Greenblatt's writing lies in his ability to connect these apparently 'known' authors to surprising and non-canonical, often non-literary materials drawn from the period in which these writers lived and wrote. Greenblatt is interested in culture in the widest sense, and this has led him to engage with some of the most pressing issues not only for the early modern period but for our contemporary world. What is the relationship between life and art? How does belief relate to imagination? How does a dominant culture cope with various kinds of 'other' (including other races or ethnicities, 'non-standard' sexualities, unorthodox religious views, political resistance, the irrational or unbelievable)? Greenblatt's work is full of ghosts, of witchcraft, of wonder and strangeness, of colonial encounters and traumatic moments in history. As the following chapters show, what is new about new historicism is in part its attention to aspects of the past that refuse to fit into established histories. It challenges the idea that history is concerned with events and situations that are somehow 'over', finished with, and safely distant from our own concerns.

What has made such new historicist work possible is an insistence on probing boundaries in Greenblatt's texts, and this includes the boundaries of literary criticism itself. Greenblatt's work draws on traditional approaches to literature and history, but it also takes on elements of anthropology, psychology, postcolonial theory, gender theory, philosophy, political thought, art history and theology. What unites these disparate materials is Greenblatt's style. His texts are

RENAISSANCE/EARLY MODERN

In this book I will be using the terms Renaissance and early modern interchangeably. Both are used to indicate a period in English literature and history that runs broadly from 1500 to 1700, although critics often disagree on exactly when such periods begin and end. It is worth thinking a little more about these terms, however, since they do have different implications. Renaissance, which literally means 'rebirth', stresses the continuities between the so-called Golden Age cultures of ancient Greece and Rome and that of England in the sixteenth and seventeenth centuries. In this sense, 'Renaissance' is a backwards-looking term. One of the consequences of this is that it can turn the intervening medieval period into the 'Dark' ages, implying that the highest forms of culture exist only on either side of it. On the other hand, to talk of an early modern period is to assert a continuity with that which comes after the Renaissance, namely modernity. Thus it points forward, and many critics prefer early modern in part because it allows them to trace the formation of modern culture in that which is described as early modern. Greenblatt uses both terms, as can be seen in the titles of his books *Renaissance Self-Fashioning* and *Learning to Curse: Essays in Early Modern Culture*.

compelling, written with a combination of thinking about overarching concepts and scrupulous attention to detail. There is humour in his work, but also a high level of seriousness about the importance of the literary and artistic works that he discusses. In his essay on 'Culture', Greenblatt gives a description of the power of language, and of those who use it, to appeal to a reader's most fundamental emotions:

> In any culture there is a general symbolic economy made up of the myriad signs that excite human desire, fear, and aggression. Through their ability to construct resonant stories, their command of effective imagery, and above all their sensitivity to the greatest collective creation of any culture – language – literary artists are skilled at manipulating this economy.

> (2005: 15)

Cultural products such as literature make something happen to their audiences, and this is partly the result of the powerful effects of language. If we were to rewrite this paragraph, changing only one word to turn 'literary artists' into 'literary critics', we might have a good indication of what it is that Greenblatt is trying to achieve in his writing. Literature and criticism both aim to demonstrate a sensitivity to language, to tell a compelling story, to create images that linger in the mind, and this brings them into contact with the 'symbolic economy' to which Greenblatt refers. Thinking about the symbolic in terms of economy allows us to see how images, objects, narratives and representations are produced, reproduced, consumed, traded and circulated, and how they change value as they move from one area of a culture to another. A good example of this would be the way in which images of the current British monarch, Queen Elizabeth II, are used in modern British culture. Representations of the Queen are used in formal portraits, on banknotes, coins, postage stamps, postcards, commemorative mugs and a huge variety of official publications and souvenirs. Yet the Queen has also become a semi-fictional character in drama, television and film, has been impersonated by comedians, and her image has been exploited by punk bands and others in their own publicity. In each case, the image is 'the same' – it is always a representation of a specific person – but this image takes on a variable status and value depending on its use, and will 'mean' different things to different people even in the case of a single usage. I will say more about these ideas of culture and economy in Chapters 1 and 2.

Literature is part of the economy of culture. Since literary works are never seen to be separate or separable from the lives and histories that are involved in their production and reception, Greenblatt's evident love of literature never blinds him to the social conditions pertaining to a text. He is equally aware of his own implication in those histories, and of his own position as a witness to those lives. In *Marvelous Possessions*, his book on the encounters between European travellers and the inhabitants and cultures of the 'New World', he tells the following anecdote:

> At the end of one of my lectures in Chicago, a student challenged me to account for my own position. How can I avoid the implication, she asked, that I have situated myself at a very safe distance from the Europeans about whom I write, a distance secured by means of a sardonic smile that protects me from implication in the discursive practices I am describing? The answer is that I do not claim such protection nor do I imagine myself situated at a safe distance.
>
> (1991: viii–ix)

He goes on to say that, in fact, *Marvelous Possessions* is partly intended to be a critique of some of the values, stemming from his Jewish Zionist upbringing, to which he still feels an uneasy attachment. His work on the early modern period and its colonial activities is thus at once both historical scholarship and an autobiographically motivated attempt to come to terms with his own contemporary position. There is a connection between the materials that he reads and the world that he inhabits, despite the temporal distance of around 400 years. Ideas, like the colonists, travel. The past is not yet finished, or finished with.

To some, no doubt, the idea of a volume on Stephen Greenblatt in a series called 'Routledge Critical Thinkers' will seem an odd one. Few would question the impact of Greenblatt's texts on a variety of fields, and no one working in literary studies in the last twenty years could have remained unaware of new historicism, the critical movement with which he has become inextricably associated, and which he is often credited with founding (or at least naming). But does this amount to being a 'critical thinker'? Part of the problem in answering this question, as we shall see in the course of this book, is to do with the characteristic modes of new historicist writing itself. New historicism tends to be thought of as a practice rather than a theory (such as Marxism, psychoanalysis, reader response, cognitive poetics, and so on). To some extent, new historicism has revived the traditional split between 'theory' and 'practice'. Consequently, unlike many of the subjects of the volumes in this series, practitioners of new historicism such as Greenblatt are rarely regarded as 'theorists'. Where names such as those of Derrida, Barthes, Foucault, Kristeva or Butler are widely known, and their works are frequently the subject of academic and occasionally non-academic discussion across several disciplines, new historicism has had an enormous impact on and beyond literary studies without elevating its main proponents to the same kind of 'star' status.

Nonetheless, Stephen Greenblatt has become the most conspicuous figure of this influential movement. His work is critical in precisely the ways that Robert Eaglestone describes in his Preface to the books in this series. Greenblatt's work is fundamentally a form of criticism. It is primarily concerned with offering readings of textual and sometimes visual material. Second, even if an overarching theoretical perspective can only be extracted from his work with some difficulty, there are certainly terms and ideas originating in Greenblatt's texts that have been taken up by many other critics, and which could be used by you. The notion of 'self-fashioning', for example, which is the central term from his first major book (and which is the subject of Chapter 3 in this book), has been employed by many critics. Third, Greenblatt has always engaged with some of the most crucial and far-reaching questions facing cultural criticism in several disciplines. The answers that his works give to these questions are thus of consequence for literary and cultural critics of every persuasion, including those who do not see themselves as historicists.

GREENBLATT'S CAREER

Stephen Jay Greenblatt was born on 7 November 1943 in Cambridge, Massachusetts, USA. He did his undergraduate and graduate work at Yale University, earning his BA in 1964, an M.Phil. in 1968 and his Ph.D. in 1969. As part of his graduate work, Greenblatt also studied at Cambridge in England, earning his M.Phil. there in 1966. For twenty-eight years he taught at the University of California, Berkeley, where he became a member of the editorial collective for the journal *Representations*, launched in 1983 and still running, in which much of the most influential work in the early days of new historicism was published. In 1997 he moved to Harvard University to become, first,

Harry Levin Professor of Literature and then, from 2000, the John Cogan University Professor of the Humanities. In the 1990s, he also became one of the General Editors of the widely used *Norton Anthology of English Literature* and General Editor of *The Norton Shakespeare*. Greenblatt has also acted as President of the Modern Language Association of America, one of the most influential professional academic bodies, has won many academic awards and prizes, and in 2005 was nominated for the prestigious Pulitzer Prize for *Will in the World*.

'NEW' HISTORICISM

What is the new historicism? Of course, as the name itself suggests, we have to take into account two aspects of that question of definition: first, we need to think about historicism, and second, what is 'new' about this version of it.

It seems sensible to start with one of the earliest formulations that Greenblatt gives of what marks out new historicism from other critical practices. In his introduction to a collection of essays that he edited in 1982, Greenblatt proposes that:

> The new historicism erodes the firm ground of both criticism and literature. It tends to ask questions about its own methodological assumptions and those of others . . . Moreover [it] has been less concerned to establish the organic unity of literary works and more open to such works as fields of force, places of dissension and shifting interests, occasions for the jostling of orthodox and subversive impulses . . . Renaissance literary works are no longer regarded as either a fixed set of texts that are set apart from all other forms of expression and that contain their own determinate meanings or as a stable set of reflections of historical facts that lie beyond them. The critical practice represented in this volume challenges the assumptions that guarantee a secure distinction between 'literary foreground' and 'political background' or, more generally between artistic production and other kinds of social production. Such distinctions do in fact exist, but they are not intrinsic to the texts; rather they are made up and constantly redrawn by artists, audiences, and readers. These collective social constructions on the one hand define the range of aesthetic possibilities within a given representational mode and, on the other, link that mode to the complex network of institutions, practices, and beliefs that constitute the culture as a whole.

(Greenblatt 1982: 5–6)

There is a great deal packed into this statement that will allow us to begin to disentangle some of the central tenets of the new historicism. First, there is the reference to the 'organic unity' of the literary text. This marks an attempt to challenge one of the key ideas of what was known as 'New Criticism'. As Catherine Gallagher and Greenblatt put it in their co-written book *Practicing New Historicism*, to them the term new historicism 'at first signified an impatience with American New Criticism, an unsettling of established norms and procedures, a mingling of dissent and restless curiosity' (Gallagher and Greenblatt 2000: 2). New Critics, as we will see in a moment, are best thought of as formalists, that is, their criticism focuses on the formal aspects of literary texts, and they characteristically find themselves demonstrating the ways in which each element of a text contributes to producing a coherent whole. In place of this coherence, new historicists pay attention to those parts of a text that seem not to fit together and that can't therefore simply be added together to make an organic whole. Taking into account these discordant elements involves thinking about the 'subversive' alongside the 'orthodox', which means that the orthodox has to be seen in a new light. In particular, in new historicist readings there is an emphasis on those parts of a text that seem to be at odds with the ways in which the period in which that text originates is usually understood. In this sense, there is also an engagement with critical understandings of history and of historical periods. It is in this double movement – exploring the ways in which texts subvert themselves, and selecting texts that undermine the historical frameworks that have conventionally been used to explain them – that the 'firm ground' of criticism is undermined.

In thinking about how new historicists read against established histories, it is worth noting something about the way in which Greenblatt talks about history as well. In place of a stable sense of objects or histories as unchanging, waiting for the critic to view them from a fixed point, Greenblatt uses words such as 'shifting' and 'jostling', verbs that connote an ongoing process. This is why he also talks of the distinctions between art and other aspects of society as being 'constantly redrawn'. Just as the world that new historicists depict is one in which there are competing and clashing forces and beliefs, so the interpretation of that world is itself a fluid and active process.

Let's return to Greenblatt's definition. The second aspect that we need to think about is the foreground/background distinction. This

NEW CRITICISM

The New Critics were a group of American literary scholars whose work dominated the critical scene from the 1930s to the 1950s, the most prominent of whom were John Crowe Ransom (1888–1974), Cleanth Brooks (1906–94), Kenneth Burke (1897–1993), Allen Tate (1899–1979) and William K. Wimsatt (1907–75). The movement drew its name from Ransom's 1941 book *The New Criticism*. Rejecting an earlier philological approach to literature that stressed the historical dimension of language change and the biography and intention of the author, New Critics aimed to show poetry as essentially self-contained and self-sustaining in terms of meaning. The reading of literature was to be impersonal, professional and concerned with the ahistorical value of the text (in fact, a text's value was, in large part, attributed to its ahistorical ability to transcend the mere history of a given moment). The central tenets of New Criticism included a desire to look at a poem as a poem as closely as possible, to see the 'text in itself' through a practice of 'close reading', emphasizing formal aspects such as irony, metaphor, paradox and conceit. Yet this quasi-scientific desire to show how a literary text works through the analysis of its formal elements – in the way that one might show how a machine works by disassembling it and examining all of its parts – runs the risk of turning the text into a dead object, and so there is also a movement to account for the effect of the text as a whole, and thus to show how all of the constituent parts work together to create the 'being' of a particular text. Unity, order, harmony and transcendence become dominant themes, and the New Critics sought to show that all of the aspects of a poem (including irony and paradox) that could be isolated would nonetheless add up to an organic whole. It is for this reason that a critic such as Brooks insists that a poem cannot be paraphrased, since paraphrase necessarily focuses on certain aspects of a poem at the expense of others. As Wimsatt puts it, the text is a 'verbal icon', equivalent to a sculpture or vase, and equal in its solidity and sense of completeness as a single object. In *Learning to Curse*, Greenblatt explicitly distances himself from Wimsatt (1992: 1–2).

refs to the idea that historical facts lie outside of the literary text, and at a distance from it. In New Criticism, the text was seen to be sufficient to itself, and didn't need external knowledge of history or society, or of the author's biography, in order to make it meaningful. One consequence of this view is that literature can have no direct influence on cultural change outside of a narrow sense of literary history.

Equally, talking about the relationship between literature and history as Greenblatt does is a deliberate attempt to state a difference between new historicist practice and older forms of historicism. When Greenblatt refers to his disagreement with the idea of a literary work 'reflecting' historical facts, he has in mind a form of criticism that too easily sees history as the 'explanation' of a text, where any problematic area in the text is read off against a context that is seen to be less ambiguous. For the new historicists, by contrast, literary texts cannot be isolated as entities that lie outside of history, such that political and social concerns are then seen as a backdrop against which the aesthetic work plays itself out. Artistic production is instead seen to be of a part with other kinds of production, although this does not mean that all forms of production are identical. Rather, there is a relationship between art and other elements within a culture, and it is for the new historicist to work out what that relationship might be. It is also necessary to take account of how artistic texts contribute to the production of that culture. In one of the most famous formulations of this doubled sense of relationship, Louis Montrose identifies a new historicist commitment to what he terms 'The Historicity of Texts and Textuality of History'. A sentence with this kind of structure – in which the second part of the sentence inverts the order of the first part, as in 'Fail to prepare, prepare to fail', and so on – is called a *chiasmus*, after the Greek letter χ (*chi*). What it attempts to do, in rhetorical terms, is to show the inseparability of the two main nouns in the sentence (text/history or preparation/failure). Glossing this comment, Montrose notes:

> The new orientation to history in Renaissance literary studies may be succinctly characterized, on the one hand, by its acknowledgment of the *historicity of texts*: the cultural specificity, the social embedment, of all modes of writing – not only those texts that critics study but also the texts in which they study them; and, on the other hand, by its acknowledgment of the *textuality of history*: the unavailability of a full and authentic past, a lived material existence, that has not already been mediated by the surviving texts of the

> society in question – those 'documents' that historians construe in their own
> texts, called 'histories', histories that necessarily but always incompletely
> construct the 'History' to which they offer access.
>
> (Montrose 1986: 8)

Greenblatt endorses this view of the general project of new historicism (1992: 170) and, like Montrose, he is influenced not only by a movement within literary studies, but within the discipline of history.

At the end of the paragraph from Montrose that I have just quoted, he includes a footnote to the work of the historian Hayden White (1928–). In a series of influential books, White proposes that history (or History) is to be thought of primarily as a form of writing, and is thus open to analysis as narrative. He pursues this line of inquiry in books such as *Metahistory* (1973), *Tropics of Discourse* (1978) and *The Content of the Form* (1987). White stresses the importance of recognizing the role that a 'historical imagination' plays in shaping historical explanation, proposing that there is always a 'metahistorical' element in historiography (the writing of history) that is poetic and linguistic in nature. Any term that includes the prefix 'meta-' implies a higher order of explanation, and, in speaking of metahistory, White means that there is always a philosophy of history that underpins the ways in which particular histories get written, and his book *Metahistory* is thus a history of history (just as a 'metalanguage' is the language that is used to explain the operations of a language). For White, historians work by *representing* the past, and these representations open up an awareness of what he calls the 'poetics' of history. (For a brief essay on new historicism by White, see Veeser 1989: 293–302.)

As will become clear in Chapters 1 and 2, it is easy to see why such an approach to history would be of interest to those pursuing cultural poetics. There are distinct affinities between Greenblatt's sense of history as not only accessible through, but also constituted by, representations and White's emphasis on a poetics of history. Both writers are interested in the ways in which formal aspects of narratives (or of literature more generally) intersect with historical understanding. What is particularly worthy of note is that White and Greenblatt share the view that historical and formal concerns are inseparable, and that analysing the writing of history (their own, and that of others) has to involve elements of formalist analysis. So while it is true that new historicism is opposed to the formalist work of the New Critics, nonetheless it is itself in part a formalist practice, avoiding the common opposition of formalism to historicism. This formal aspect could also be one of the reasons that Greenblatt has on the whole preferred 'cultural poetics' as a description of his work, since the inclusion of the term 'poetics' makes clear the formal dimension.

Trying to sum up some of the principles of new historicism, H. Aram Veeser proposes the following:

1. that every expressive act is embedded in a network of material practices;
2. that every act of unmasking, critique, and opposition uses the tools it condemns and risks falling prey to the practice it exposes;
3. that literary and non-literary 'texts' circulate inseparably;
4. that no discourse, imaginative or archival, gives access to unchanging truths nor expresses inalterable human nature;
5. finally, . . . that a critical method and a language adequate to describe culture under capitalism participate in the economy they describe.

(Veeser 1989: xi)

Some of these ideas will be familiar from what I have already said about new historicism, others will become clearer as you read the 'Key Ideas' chapters. For now, let us just focus on some of the main points. First, there is the sense of connection between an 'expressive act' and other practices within a culture. In describing expression, Veeser is careful not to limit this to a conventional notion of literary texts, and this is reinforced in point 3. Second, Veeser gives a sense of the purpose of new historicist reading, and of what it may look for in the texts of earlier periods, when he refers to acts of unmasking, critique and opposition. There is no sense here that criticism is neutral, or that critics might be interested in reading or writing texts that describe or reinforce the dominant value systems of a culture. But he also raises a difficulty. Because criticism is a practice that is also part of a culture, and because it might have to use the same 'tools' as those to whom it is opposed, there is always the potential to end up reinforcing dominant values even if the intention is to oppose them. This should alert us to how the critic presents ideas, not just what he or she says. Point 5 makes this explicit. Point 4 echoes the idea that any discourse – again, Veeser is talking about more than just literature – is the product of, and impacts on, a specific moment in history, and doesn't reveal a transhistorical sense of truth or human nature, that is, something that would be true for any person, in any culture, at any point in history.

One question remains, however. Is this in itself 'new'? It is true to say that, like any critical practice, the new historicism didn't come from nowhere. There were critics who were working in a mode that might now be thought of as new historicist before the term itself was invented. Prominent among scholars of Renaissance literature would be Stephen Orgel and J. W. Lever, both of whom wrote books in the 1970s that shared many of the preoccupations of the new historicists who followed (see Orgel 1975 and Lever 1971). What new historicism did was to engage more explicitly with critical 'theory', especially with the work of thinkers such as Michel Foucault, while at the same time retaining many of the traditional aspects of literary criticism. One way of judging the newness of the new historicism, however, is to note the hostile reception that it received in its early years. Some critics saw it as a radical and threatening form of Marxism (see Pechter 1995), while others decried it as conservative. Even if new historicism had only been a combination of already existing approaches to literary study, it was nonetheless taken as a troubling movement that had to be countered. As Gallagher notes: 'the new historicism attracts an unusual amount of specifically political criticism for a criticism whose politics are so difficult to specify' (Gallagher in Veeser 1989: 37). As I will show in the chapters that follow, defining and responding to the new historicism has often been a matter of trying to make it fit within established categories (Left v. Right, liberatory v. regressive, and so on). One of its defining features, however, has been its refusal to fit cleanly into such categories. This makes the question of the newness of new historicism a tricky one. Has it radically changed the state of literary studies, using the word radical in its etymological sense of going down to the roots? Has it simply reinforced ideas that were already present within literary criticism and is thus new only in the way that advertisements use the label 'new and improved' as a way to sell us the same old products? More importantly, are we in a position yet to say what new historicism will turn out to have been? This last question is one to which I will return, particularly in the 'After Greenblatt' chapter.

THIS BOOK

The discussion in this chapter is designed to outline some of the main reasons why you might want to continue reading this book. The account of new historicism, and of Greenblatt's work in particular, will be developed as the book progresses, and many of the ideas that have been quickly sketched in here will be given more detailed treatment in the 'Key Ideas' section. In 'Key Ideas', I take the idea of 'idea' in two ways. Chapters 1 and 2 address the broad concepts, such as culture and cultural poetics, to be found in Greenblatt's work, and that have been most influential on other critics. These two chapters offer an overview that refers to texts from across Greenblatt's career. The second part of this section, Chapters 3 to 6, looks at the most crucial ideas for understanding particular texts, including self-fashioning, social energy, wonder, and imagination. What emerges from this latter part is a broadly chronological sense of Greenblatt's work, and an indication of how to read the particular discussions in his main books.

One of the other reasons that 'Why Greenblatt?' remains, and must remain, a difficult question to answer stems from the fact that Stephen Greenblatt is, as I write this, still alive. He will, I hope, live for many years. He will, I hope, write several more books. By the time this book appears, he will have published work that it will necessarily have been impossible for me to take into account. This won't, then, be a complete guide to Greenblatt's work, just as it isn't possible for me to give a complete sense of his life in this chapter, but it should give you ways into reading his work for yourself, including the work that is still to come.

KEY IDEAS

1

FROM CULTURE TO
CULTURAL POETICS

Central to the new historicist project is the notion that literature is related to other practices, behaviour and values, and that literature is thus always in relation to the non-literary. Consequently, the definition of culture, and of how different aspects of a culture relate to each other, becomes of prime importance in understanding Greenblatt's work. In this chapter, I will begin by discussing Greenblatt's sense of culture, and then move on to see how this informs cultural materialism and cultural poetics.

'CULTURE'

At the beginning of a short essay originally published in 1990 as an entry in a dictionary of critical terms for literary study, Stephen Greenblatt asks why a concept of 'Culture' should be useful to students of literature (Greenblatt 2005: 11). Disconcertingly, his initial answer is to suggest that it might not be. Part of the problem lies in the vagueness of the word. What does it include? Everything? In which case, it is not of much use as a descriptive term. But if it refers instead to a more limited conception of social structures, productions or interactions, then what is to be included and what excluded?

Greenblatt's recognition of the difficulties that surround the concept of culture is shared by one of his critical influences. When Raymond

Williams comes to define the term in his book *Keywords*, he opens by
suggesting that:

> Culture is one of the two or three most complicated words in the English
> language. This is so partly because of its intricate historical development, in
> several European languages, but mainly because it has now come to be used
> for important concepts in several distinct intellectual disciplines and in several
> distinct and incompatible systems of thought.

(1983: 87)

The repeated use of the word 'several' gives a clue to the problem.
It is not just that the word is vague in itself, it is also that it has come
to mean many different things within different contexts. Context here
does not just refer to changes over time, although that 'historical
development' is a factor, but also to the varied senses of the word
within different languages and to the different disciplines which have
employed it within one language. Precisely because it is a term that
has eluded precise definition, or which has always been open to multiple
definitions, it has been used within areas as diverse as literary studies,
art history, sociology, anthropology, history, philosophy, cultural studies
(about which more in a moment), and so on, but in ways that differ
in each case. This is further complicated by the fact that these discipline-
specific meanings are not compatible with each other, so they cannot
just be added together to arrive at a more complete sense of the term.
The struggle to define culture continues, and some of the difficulties
are very ably summarized in another recent attempt to work out its
critical significance (see Bruster 2003).

In trying to define the concept of culture, then, Greenblatt is forced
to begin by making some broad distinctions. The concept refers to
two opposing ideas, which he calls *constraint* and *mobility*. On the one
hand, there is the set of beliefs and practices, frequently backed up
by institutions and a 'technology of control', that sets limits on the
behaviour of individuals. By 'technology', Greenblatt does not mean
the most common modern use of the word which would make us think
of gadgets or machines that allow people to be observed and thus
controlled, such as CCTV. He is using the word in a way that echoes
the Greek word *technē*, from which 'technology' derives. *Technē* is
closer to technique, it really means what we now call an 'art', in the
sense of phrases such as 'the art of war' or 'the art of diplomacy'.

RAYMOND WILLIAMS (1921–88)

Williams was one of the most prominent figures in the New Left within Britain in the middle decades of the twentieth century, teaching both in adult education and later at Cambridge University. His work influenced both literary and cultural studies, and his most significant books include *Culture and Society 1780–1950* (1958), *The Long Revolution* (1961), *Keywords: A Vocabulary of Culture and Society* (1976) and *Marxism and Literature* (1977). The last book, in particular, outlined his notion of cultural materialism (which will be discussed later in this chapter). As a Marxist thinker, Williams emphasized the relationships between politics and literature, focusing on concepts such as ideology and hegemony, but remaining sceptical about many of their traditional definitions. Indeed, the project of works such as *Culture and Society*, *Keywords* and *Marxism and Literature* was explicitly to examine the development of the definitions of major concepts, recognizing the often radical changes in meaning that occur over time. On Williams, see Gallagher and Greenblatt 2000: 60–66.

While the limits placed on an individual's behaviour need not be narrow or obvious in everyday life, the rules that govern social interaction are not infinitely flexible. It is clear in cases where people break the law and are punished where these limits lie, but Greenblatt suggests that they may also be seen in less dramatic gestures such as signs of disapproval from those around us. Equally, there is positive reinforcement of these limits through the reward of behaviour that is deemed appropriate. In these instances of disapproval or reward, there is not necessarily any direct sense of a disciplining power at work; it is not a matter of policing or legal enforcement. Instead, what these ideas suggest is that people at any level of society may play an active (if not always fully conscious) part in exercising control over others within the same society. We might understand this better by thinking about the phrase 'law and order'. Law tends to be exercised from above, and by those empowered to do so (the police, lawyers, judges, and so on). Order, however, is less overt in its manifestations, and most of the time there is order simply because people choose to behave in a way which does not call for any control. In other words, order might be thought of as the result of society exercising self-control.

This is all contained in the idea of constraint, but it is also where Greenblatt makes the first link to literature. Literature, he proposes, is part of this cultural reinforcement of boundaries between that which is approved and not, that which is legitimate and not, that which is legal and not. This is most obviously apparent in the praise and blame that is to be found in literary genres such as satire and panegyric. Both genres tend to emphasize, for good or ill, particular actions or modes

MICHEL FOUCAULT (1926-84)

One of the most influential of the thinkers associated with French structuralism and poststructuralism, Foucault's work has had a profound influence on several disciplines. In part this is because his own work was always determinedly interdisciplinary. His most famous works include *The Order of Things* (1966), *Discipline and Punish* (1975) and the three-volume *The History of Sexuality* (1976, 1984, 1984). Foucault sought to understand the processes by which both the objects of knowledge and the questions that we ask of those objects come into being. At the Collège de France, he was elected to a Chair (Professorship) in the History of Systems of Thought, and this title is a good way to characterize his interests. In books that investigate categories such as madness or sexuality, or the history of the hospital and of the prison, Foucault analyses the discourses that determine why a particular issue or topic is necessarily thought of in a particular way at a specific moment in history. He is interested in why the attitude expressed in texts (including literary texts), or in the functioning of an institution such as a prison, seems to be part of a collective view rather than just the opinion of a given individual. Central to Foucault's work is the notion that knowledge is always a form of power. Thus advances in psychiatry or in the treatment of illnesses also lead to new ways of controlling the people who are categorized as mad or ill. Such control tends to reinforce the power of those in a position to impose the categories. But this does not mean that power is simply exercised from the top down. As Foucault puts it: 'Power is everywhere; not because it embraces everything, but because it comes from everywhere' (1990: 93). Systems of thought are part of this process of control, and so ideas are implicated in power. Foucault's thinking also implies that working out why ideas appear in a specific form at a specific moment gives us the opportunity to think how something might be thought of in a different manner.

of conduct. In a satire, individuals or groups are held up to ridicule, but usually for specific reasons, and these reasons may give us an indication of the values of the writer, of the writer's group, or of the intended audience. Of course, the more local references to, for example, a political figure or event become of less interest over time, in that their initial force will inevitably diminish as the issue at stake becomes less urgent. So jokes about the Falklands War or Napoleon or one of the favourites of Elizabeth I might not seem to have much of a cutting edge for a modern reader, although they might still be funny. But it might be possible for us still to 'get' the more serious aspects of the joke if we are able to work out why it seemed so challenging or shocking at the time it was written, and to whom.

We need to be clear about what Greenblatt is saying here. Part of the clue as to how to interpret this essay is given by looking to the terminology that he uses. Greenblatt's use of concepts such as 'technology', 'discipline', 'punishment', and so on, is heavily influenced by the work of Michel Foucault. In thinking about questions of law and order, and in suggesting that order is part of the political organization of a culture, Greenblatt echoes Foucault: 'The state is by itself an order of things . . . Political knowledge deals not with the rights of people or with human and divine laws but with the nature of the state which has to be governed' (Foucault 2002: 408). At a specific point in time, that is, within a particular culture, there will be techniques that govern the relationships between individuals and social entities, and these techniques can be analysed to give us a sense of the nature of a state.

In the light of his sense of literature's role in the technologies of control within a society, Greenblatt outlines a series of questions that he thinks it appropriate to ask of literary works:

What kinds of behavior, what models of practice, does this work seem to enforce?

Why might readers at a particular time and place find this work compelling?

Are there differences between my values and the values implicit in the work I am reading?

Upon what social understandings does the work depend?

Whose freedom of thought or movement might be constrained implicitly or explicitly by this work?

What are the larger social structures with which these particular acts of praise or blame might be connected?

(2005: 12)

Much of this points to the world or culture beyond the text, drawing literature into a series of connections with institutions and values that are not themselves strictly literary. But this should not, Greenblatt proposes, mean that we ignore the formal characteristics of texts, or forego traditional literary practices of close reading in favour of historical and cultural description. This might seem to maintain a distinction between the formal aspects of a literary work, which we might want to call its textuality, and the contextual elements that frame the text. Yet again, however, this notion of close reading takes us back to culture, since Greenblatt proposes that 'texts are not merely cultural by virtue of reference to the world beyond themselves; they are cultural by virtue of social values and contexts that they have themselves successfully absorbed' (2005: 12). Context, then, is not a background to the text, or a frame within which it may be read. Cultural contexts are not outside the text, but are absorbed into it, and it is this process of absorption that explains the persistence of works of art outside of the contexts in which they are originally produced.

Fundamental to this view of the relation between text and culture, then, is a refusal to allow any rigid distinction between the inside and the outside of a work. To study literature is to study culture but, conversely, to understand literature, we have to understand a culture. Literary study is of value in this account because it leads to a fuller cultural understanding but, equally, it is this understanding of culture that informs the reading of the literary text. There may appear to be a certain circularity to this explanation, but it is better to think of it as another version of the *chiasmus* that I quoted from Louis Montrose in the 'Why Greenblatt?' chapter. Greenblatt's thinking here may be rendered as: culture produces literature and literature produces culture. Thinking of literature in terms of culture allows the critic to see the ways in which culture may be seen as both inside and outside literature.

For the moment, we need to return to Greenblatt's dualistic sense of culture as both constraint and mobility. Alongside the reinforcement of boundaries, he suggests, culture is also what gives structure to movement. Boundaries only become meaningful if there is also mobility, if there is a possibility of their being crossed, and Greenblatt talks of this in the 'Culture' essay primarily in terms of 'improvisation' (a key term in *Renaissance Self-Fashioning*. See Chapter 3). What does he mean by improvisation? Most obviously, it refers to the ways in which individuals accommodate themselves to their cultural constraints. It is a structure of improvisation that provides a 'set of patterns that have enough elasticity, enough scope for variation, to accommodate most of the participants in a given culture' (2005: 14). Most people will thus be able to find a manner of conforming to imposed restrictions, often without even noticing that these boundaries are in place. After all, a constraint is only experienced as such in the attempt (however unwitting) to perform an action that the constraint is designed to disallow. Without the freedom to encounter a boundary, there is no way in which the boundary may be perceived. One of the functions of literature is to present improvisation as something to be learned. In other words, the process of coming to terms with the limits on social behaviour may be portrayed in a novel, for example, as part of the process of becoming 'cultured'. By showing a character who encounters difficulties but is in the end reconciled to his or her cultural constraints, a literary text may explore thematically the process of which it is itself a part.

Literature offers a clear example of how this improvisation works. Not only are there social values which will either be reinforced or challenged by the content of a work, there are also specifically literary boundaries which have to be negotiated, such as generic conventions. The negotiation of literary boundaries entails a borrowing from the materials available in a culture at any given time. No writer begins with a clean slate, and each must form a work in the light of existing narratives, plots, linguistic resources and prior treatments of particular themes and ideas. What we think of as 'great' writers are those who most effectively engage in a process of cultural 'exchange', taking an existing item such as a familiar myth, symbol or character type and transforming it into something else, usually through an alteration in its context or by combining it with materials from another, often unexpected, source. There are many examples of this in literature, including the plays of Shakespeare, John Milton's *Paradise Lost*, James Joyce's *Ulysses*, Jean Rhys' *Wide Sargasso Sea* or J. M. Coetzee's *Foe*. Consequently, rather than being evidence of the originality or genius of a particularly gifted individual (both of which are privileged in our inheritance from romanticism), works of art 'are structures for the accumulation, transformation, representation, and communication of *social* energies and practices' (2005: 15, my emphasis). ('Social energy' is another of Greenblatt's key terms, used most frequently in *Shakespearean Negotiations*. See Chapter 4.) It is common to think of an

author as the origin of a text, as if the writer begins with a blank piece
of paper or canvas and conjures up something unique and uniquely his
(since the term genius is nearly always associated with a male writer
or artist). So someone who creates a work of art comes to be seen as
a special kind of person, either because he is able to produce something
that ordinary people are not, or else because he is directly 'inspired'
and his work transcends the ordinary world. As the English romantic
poet Percy Bysshe Shelley puts it in 'A Defence of Poetry' (2002:
513): 'A Poet participates in the eternal, the infinite and the one; as
far as relates to his conceptions, time and place and number are not.'
It is exactly this sense of the eternal or infinite, beyond time and place,
that Greenblatt challenges. For him, a poet's 'conceptions' (that is, his
ideas) are firmly grounded in the culture in which he lives and works,
in a specific time and place, and so is the art that he produces (which
we might also think of as 'conceptions' if we follow the sense of
'that which is conceived', as we say of children). The work of art in
Greenblatt's model thus situates itself somewhere between the two
poles of production and reception. Stressing neither the creativity of
the author, nor the imaginative engagement of the reader, Greenblatt
here emphasizes accumulation, transformation, representation and
communication. The artwork draws from the culture in which it
emerges, but it also reproduces that culture in a modified form that
can travel, across the boundaries within a culture, between cultures,
and across time.

What Greenblatt calls for in this brief essay is a combination of
reading practices, informed both by history and by a sense of the aesthetic
and formal dimensions of literary texts, in which it is possible to
see the relation of a text to that which seemingly lies outside it. This
presents a problem for the critic, in that he or she must be able to
handle materials more usually thought of as the domain of historians,
but must not relinquish the strengths of analysis of those materials that
are literary-critical in nature. Thus the point is not to become a historian,
since there is still a crucial aspect of the experience of literature that
makes it necessary to retain critical reading as a skill. In other words,
there is still something about literature as art that makes it different
from other kinds of historical documents:

> For great works of art are not neural relay stations in the circulation of cultural
> materials. Something happens to objects, beliefs, and practices when they are

represented, reimagined, and performed in literary texts, something often
unpredictable and disturbing. That 'something' is the sign both of the power
of art and of the embeddedness of culture in the contingencies of history.

(2005: 16)

The accumulation of cultural materials that characterizes the artwork
does not make it simply a receptacle into which ideas, energies and
practices are poured. Those materials are transformed in the artwork,
and it is this transformation that is represented and communicated along
with the 'original' sources. The critic must, therefore, try to be aware
not only of the ways in which a historical context might have contributed
to the shaping of the work of art, he or she must also be sensitive to
the transformations of that context that the artwork may perform.

CULTURAL STUDIES

By encouraging his readers to move beyond ideas of literary texts
closed off from other aspects of the culture in which they originated,
Greenblatt moves literary criticism closer to a form of cultural studies.
In his own works, Greenblatt discusses various kinds of literary and
non-literary texts, ritual, painting and architecture, and his critical
stance draws upon literary criticism, history, anthropology, politics,
philosophy, psychoanalysis and theology.

Is Greenblatt's practice, then, a kind of cultural studies? Perhaps
predictably, the answer is 'yes and no'. The history of Cultural Studies
as a discipline does not give us a single definition of its purposes and
practices, but it is possible to discern some clear threads. Beginning
with the Centre for Contemporary Cultural Studies, which emerged
at Birmingham University in England in 1964 as an offshoot of the
English Department, the British strand of cultural studies was heavily
influenced by Raymond Williams and sought to promote the importance
of 'ordinary' or 'popular' culture as a subject of academic scrutiny.
One of Williams's most influential statements was the proposal that
'culture is ordinary'. Coupled with an increased engagement with
Continental philosophy, cultural studies expanded its scope beyond the
contemporary and the traces of its roots in English studies faded. Cultural
studies developed concerns with issues such as ideology, race, identity,
colonialism, sexuality, genders and subcultures, and these interests are
shared with the new historicism. The impact of cultural studies has

been very broad, leading to the emergence of cultural studies itself as a specific discipline, but also blurring distinctions with other disciplines, especially literary studies. As Marjorie Garber comments: 'In one sense cultural studies is so ubiquitous that it is virtually invisible as a category' (2003: 47). Like culture, cultural studies is now ordinary.

As cultural studies has matured into being a discipline, it has moved away from its connections to literary studies. Many practitioners of it have no real interest in literature, and this marks a distinct difference from new historicism. In the end, new historicists such as Stephen Greenblatt always come back to a text, and often a canonical text such as one of Shakespeare's plays. Greenblatt's own attitude to cultural studies is complex and it relates to the questions of boundaries that we have already seen. He is led in two distinct directions, confessing that he wished 'to erase all boundaries separating cultural studies in narrowly specialized compartments', but recognizing at the same time that 'boundaries, provided they are permeable and negotiable, are useful things to think with' (Greenblatt 1992: 4–5). This is another reason for holding on to the specifically literary critical – that is, formal – aspects of traditional literary studies, even, or especially, in an era in which cultural studies is so pervasive.

CULTURAL MATERIALISM

As we have already seen, 'cultural materialism' is a term derived from the work of Raymond Williams. Its particular significance here is that in the 1980s it became a movement within literary criticism which paralleled the new historicism. Indeed, *Political Shakespeare*, the text which provided a manifesto for cultural materialism, included Stephen Greenblatt's 'Invisible Bullets' essay. What, then, is cultural materialism?

Like any critical movement, it is unwise to define it in too narrow terms, since the work produced by those brought together under this heading is diverse. Indeed, cultural materialism has been especially resistant to categorization, leading Robert Young to propose that the term 'really only amounts to a way of describing British ex-Marxists' (Young 1990: 88). In the preface to the original 1985 edition of *Political Shakespeare*, the editors offer a more forceful definition of their project:

> our belief is that a combination of historical context, theoretical method, political commitment and textual analysis offers the strongest challenge [to traditional

literary criticism] and has already contributed substantial work. Historical context undermines the transcendent significance traditionally accorded to the literary text and allows us to recover its histories; theoretical method detaches the text from immanent criticism which seeks only to reproduce it in its own terms; socialist and feminist commitment confronts the conservative categories in which most criticism has hitherto been conducted; textual analysis locates the critique of traditional approaches where it cannot be ignored. We call this 'cultural materialism'.

(Dollimore and Sinfield 1994: vii)

There are, then, four elements to cultural materialism as defined here: exploring historical context, employing theoretical method, expressing political commitment and grounding arguments in textual analysis. As in new historicism, history is used to undermine traditional literary criticism. The theoretical concerns of cultural materialism are made explicit, as is an affiliation to socialism and feminism. But the formalist element of literary criticism is also retained, not least because this allows cultural materialists to challenge traditional critics on what has historically been their own ground. Note also the tone in which this is expressed. There is a sense of radicalism, of challenge, commitment and critique. The declared purpose of such criticism is not to produce more readings of texts but, instead, to counter traditional readings through a materialist approach to culture. Political commitment is not 'added' to cultural materialist readings of texts, since traditional criticism is also seen to be political, rather than neutral or disinterested, and a challenge to traditional readings is seen to be a challenge to the politics of those readings.

Jonathan Dollimore's introduction to *Political Shakespeare* similarly makes explicit some of the connections between new historicism and cultural materialism, explaining a shared emergence from 'the convergence of history, sociology and English in cultural studies, some of the major developments in feminism, as well as continental Marxist-structuralist and post-structuralist theory, especially that of Althusser, Macherey, Gramsci and Foucault' (Dollimore and Sinfield 1994: 2–3). Dollimore does also note a crucial divergence between the two movements, however. Karl Marx famously wrote that: 'Men make their own history, but not of their own free will; not under circumstances they themselves have chosen but under the given and inherited circumstances with which they are directly confronted' (Marx 1992: 146).

MATERIALISM

Materialism has a long philosophical history and covers a variety of critical positions, but it is being used by Dollimore and Sinfield here in a sense that is most obviously related to the Marxist idea of 'historical materialism'. Put at its simplest, historical materialism is opposed to the notion that human life is determined by consciousness. The forces that shape people's lives are thus located not in ideas, interpretations or the sense that people make of the world, but are instead the product of material and social conditions such as the economic, legal, and political structures that determine the relationships between different groups in society. As such, it is opposed to 'idealism', in which the role of human consciousness and perception is stressed in the appearance of objects. Historical materialism thus strives to open up a space between our sense of the world and the realities of our existence, allowing for a critical relation to that space to emerge.

In reading this statement, where we choose to put the emphasis – on the making or on the circumstances – can be crucial. As Dollimore puts it, 'Perhaps the most significant divergence within cultural analysis is that between those who concentrate on culture as this making of history, and those who concentrate on the unchosen conditions which constrain and inform that process of making' (Dollimore and Sinfield 1994: 3). At stake is the question of agency. Greenblatt's emphasis on the relationship between constraint and mobility can be read in this light, and, as he himself admits in the 'Culture' essay: 'I have written at moments as if art always reinforces the dominant beliefs and social structures of its culture' (2005: 16). This is perhaps a response to the criticisms of the 'subversion and containment' model that several readers found in his work (see Chapter 4 where this is discussed in more detail).

While clearly inspired by Marxism, cultural materialism has steadily moved away from a more traditional emphasis on ideology critique and class relations towards the concerns that Dollimore alludes to and that *Political Shakespeare* contains: feminism, postcolonialism, gender and queer theories, and institutional critique. Alongside the readings of Shakespeare's plays, *Political Shakespeare* also contains essays on educational and economic policies, theatrical institutions such as the Royal Shakespeare Company, film and television adaptations of plays, and the relationship between Shakespeare and the tourism or 'heritage' industry. There is a strong emphasis in cultural materialism on an engagement with the present, and much of the prominent work which emerged in the 1980s explicitly responded to the policies and actions of the Right-wing government of Margaret Thatcher that was in power in Britain in those years. Such attention to contemporary concerns laid the foundations for the current move towards 'presentism' in Shakespeare studies, which will be discussed in the 'After Greenblatt' chapter of this book.

'TOWARDS A POETICS OF CULTURE'

Let's return to the quotation that we saw in the 'Why Greenblatt?' chapter of this book. In his introduction to the volume on genre, Greenblatt offered a description that took us from new historicism to his preferred term, the 'poetics of culture'. If you re-read this quotation (on p. 6), then you will be able to see how our sense of new historicism is beginning to develop. Many of the key ideas that we have already seen – criticism as a practice rather than a theory, the interplay of the orthodox and the subversive, the refusal to make a clear distinction between the inside and outside of a text, the emphasis on production, construction and constitution – are all here. But, last time, I discussed this as a definition of new historicism. What is added by thinking about it instead as the outline for a poetics of culture?

One way of assessing this would be to think about how the idea of poetics modifies our sense of culture in this phrase. It makes us aware of culture as itself constructed, as something to be made (echoing the Greek term *poiesis*, which refers to making). But equally, as the product of a form of making, culture is related to other practices and to the systems of thought that govern production. To begin to show how this works in practice, I will turn to another essay which contains both a methodological element and an example of Greenblatt's analysis at work. In the next chapter I will look in more detail at some of the characteristic modes of writing and argumentation employed by Greenblatt in his practice of cultural poetics.

The essay 'Towards a Poetics of Culture', which was first given as a lecture in 1986, begins with a somewhat perplexed account of the popularity of the term 'new historicism'. But the central purpose of the essay is to distinguish between the practice that Greenblatt employs and two alternatives: Marxism and poststructuralism. While the impact of Marxist thought on Greenblatt's work is undeniable – and undenied – this essay contains a brief anecdote that tells of a shift towards cultural poetics that stemmed precisely from a discomfort with being asked to identify exactly what kind of Marxist he was. So rather than choosing to be a particular brand of Marxist, Greenblatt gave up teaching courses with titles such as 'Marxist Aesthetics' and opted for the less problematic 'Cultural Poetics'. This is, perhaps, another example of unease regarding the rigid demarcations of boundaries and of areas of thought and culture, and Greenblatt characteristically avoids what is felt to be the false choice of an either/or in favour of a term that refuses the distinction.

In this essay, Greenblatt focuses on the work of two thinkers who he cites as examples of two critical modes, Fredric Jameson (Marxism) and Jean-François Lyotard (poststructuralism). Focusing on their attitudes towards capitalism, Greenblatt outlines the ways in which their theoretical projects (as he reads them) lead them to provide conflicting accounts of the effects of capitalism, both of which he feels to be inadequate. For Jameson, capitalism produces a division of the world, and is the agent of a 'repressive differentiation' that draws rigid distinctions between public and private, individual and society, and so on, and that produces a sense of dislocation and alienation from other people. On the other hand, Lyotard's interpretation of capitalism is exactly the opposite, in which capitalism has a flattening effect on difference and is seen to engender a 'monological totalization' in which distinctions disappear into a single and homogeneous whole (Greenblatt 1992: 151). Greenblatt proposes that the differences between their readings is not just an indication of the incompatibility of Marxism and poststructuralism, but also reveals 'the inability of either of the theories to come to terms with the apparently contradictory historical effects of capitalism' (1992: 151). In this sense, neither Jameson nor Lyotard is wrong, but both of their theories are inadequate in that they are unable to see that capitalism functions by doing two contradictory things simultaneously.

Both Jameson and Lyotard are important figures for Greenblatt because they exemplify critical positions that are frequently associated with new historicism itself. It was Jameson who came up with the slogan 'always historicize' in *The Political Unconscious* (see Jameson 2002: ix), which has been taken as a rallying cry for the historicist enterprise. Jameson is also one of the most prominent Marxist thinkers in America, and new historicism is certainly informed by Marxism. Lyotard, one of the leading French thinkers of the twentieth century, is often aligned with figures such as Foucault, whose work was instrumental in shifting from the older, positivist historicism to the newer cultural poetics. In selecting these two figures, Greenblatt is able to mark the distance between his own practice and the ideas of those with which it is linked, primarily by some of his opponents. Influenced by both Marxist thought and poststructuralism, cultural poetics is ultimately neither of these things.

To support his case, Greenblatt then goes on to examine three examples: the Presidency of Ronald Reagan (1911–2004, President 1981–89); the packaging of Yosemite National Park; and Norman Mailer's fictionalization of the case of the convicted murderer Gary Gilmore, in *Executioner's Song*. At stake in each example is the relationship between art – or at least materials usually thought to exist within an aesthetic realm – and the 'reality' of a historical or social realm. So Reagan's tendency to use lines from films (including films in which he had acted) in his political speeches as President is aligned with the framing of a view at Yosemite, which is, in turn, related to the complex interplay between Mailer's 'fictions' and the people and events with which those fictions were entangled. Stressing the negotiation of the aesthetic with the social, Greenblatt emphasizes both the appropriation of the aesthetic (as in Reagan's apparent failure to distinguish between the political discourse of a Presidential speech and the fictional lines spoken in a movie) and the exchanges that take place when some form of profit – either as money or as pleasure – is produced by an aesthetic discourse. Ultimately, Greenblatt argues, both the traditional terms that we use to talk about art (such as mimesis, allegory, symbol and representation) and the theoretical frameworks of interpretation offered by the Marxism of Jameson or the poststructuralism of Lyotard seem too limited to be able to account for the examples that he uses. Only a cultural poetics that is able to combine a historically specific attention to the shifting senses of our critical terminology with a sensitivity to aesthetic considerations will be able to map these negotiations, circulations and exchanges. In other words, if we come to an object that has an aesthetic dimension with a set of preconceptions that govern how we view the relationship between art and non-art (whether that is reality, politics, nature, capitalism, and so on), then we run the risk of failing to see what this specific aesthetic dimension is doing in, or to, that relationship. The cultural aspect of cultural poetics allows for a recognition of the specific location of a given artwork in space and time; the poetic element opens up the possibility of seeing what the artwork makes happen in that location.

SUMMARY

This chapter explores the centrality of the concept of culture in Greenblatt's work, tracing this through to the practice that he calls cultural poetics. Attending to culture allows for literary works to be connected to the contexts in which they appear in ways that blur the traditional boundaries between what is 'inside' and 'outside' a text. Connecting literary production to other forms of production, Greenblatt also stresses the specific role of the aesthetic in transforming culture. No longer the preserve of an elite (as in the idea of 'high' culture), culture is ordinary, but it is also capable of the extraordinary, surprising and delighting the critic who is sensitive to its unpredictability. Such an approach leads towards cultural studies, but the new historicist always retains a sense of the literary as a particular aesthetic domain. Many of these concerns are shared with the parallel British historicist movement that went under the name of cultural materialism. What emerges most clearly from Greenblatt's use of the term culture is an emphasis on reading texts and their specific historical circumstances rather than using an overarching theory. A sense of culture must be supplemented by an attention to poetics, and the terms of poetics are always located in culture.

2

PRACTISING
CULTURAL POETICS

Perhaps the most compelling dimension of Stephen Greenblatt's work is its style. By this I mean not merely the seductive power of his prose, although that has certainly contributed to the popularity and influence of his work, but also the structures and patterns of argument that he employs in his writings. Because, as I have suggested, Greenblatt tends to eschew bald statements of methodological or theoretical intent, his texts demand a close attention to the ways in which he presents material, and are frequently resistant to summarization. Nevertheless, it is possible to isolate features of his texts that have become central to the new historicist mode of criticism. Consequently, I will have to focus in this chapter on cultural poetics not as a type of reading but as a way of writing.

STORY-TELLING

Greenblatt's work is full of stories. Alongside the historical narratives that we might expect, there are also more personal, often autobiographical stories, most obviously at the beginnings and ends of his books. Greenblatt notes that he has a 'will to tell stories, critical stories or stories told as a form of criticism' (1992: 5). Many of these stories take the form of anecdotes, and I will turn to the anecdote and its significance in a moment. But it is worth considering first of all this impulse towards narrative, this sense that the story is somehow necessary and compelling.

In the introduction to *Learning to Curse*, Greenblatt gives a very personal sense of this narrative compulsion. First, he relates his own attachment to stories as the product of his relationship to his parents, in the narrations that his mother gave of his own life or in the tales that his father would tell. From the stories that gave him an early sense of his own 'self', there is a shift in emphasis that takes place when he considers his father's stories, and there is no longer the same confidence in narrative as a confirmation of identity. Greenblatt notes that in his father's narratives he could discern:

> a strategic way of turning disappointment, anger, rivalry, and a sense of menace into comic pleasure, a way of re-establishing the self on the site of its threatened loss. But there was an underside to this strategy that I have hinted at by calling his stories obsessive. For the stories in some sense *were* the loss of identity which they were meant to ward off – there was something compulsive about them, as if someone were standing outside of my father and insisting that he endlessly recite his tales.

> (1992: 7)

Story-telling, then, is a mode of narration that seems to pull in two directions at once. It may be used as a way to shore up a sense of self, to relate oneself to the world by relating or hearing a story about one's place in that world. But, on the other hand, to tell a story might act as an attempt to assert an identity that the stories told, by virtue of being repeated, repeatedly fail to secure. Rather than the expression of one's own will, the story seems to be the product of a demand placed upon the teller by another (or an other). As I have already shown in relation to Greenblatt's work, there is a sense in which the boundaries between 'inside' and 'outside' refuse to be fixed or stable.

This compulsive quality is not simply to be understood as a personal trait of Greenblatt's father. Rather, it seems to be a characteristic of narrative and the ways in which it is produced and consumed. Greenblatt suggests that there are two forms of regulation that govern the production and consumption of narrative; the first is an aesthetic one, including the features that determine whether a story is a good or bad one, whether it produces pleasure, and so on, and the other is psychic. This psychic regulation is exemplified in an anecdote that Greenblatt gives, in which he went through a period of intense discomfort as he felt impelled to narrate his every thought and action. The division that this set up between his sense of himself as an 'I' who had found his place in the world through stories and an ironically detached internal voice that compulsively turned him into a 'he', led to a desire for critical distance from narrative. Greenblatt notes:

> I could not endure the compulsive estrangement of my life, as if it belonged to someone else, but I could perhaps understand the uncanny otherness of my own voice, make it comprehensible and bring it under rational control by trying to understand the way in which all voices come to be woven out of strands of alien experience. I am committed to the project of making strange what has become familiar, of demonstrating that what seems an untroubling and untroubled part of ourselves (for example, Shakespeare) is actually part of something else, something different.
>
> (1992: 8)

Greenblatt moves quickly from the personal anecdote to the critical project; the experience of estrangement leads to an insight regarding the nature of voice, and this is expressed in the first person, reasserting the importance in this of the 'I' who speaks. No longer simply self-expression, however, voice is revealed as dependent upon an uncanny otherness. Just as the telling of his stories seemed to be imposed upon his father by an external force, so Greenblatt came to feel a similar sense of compulsion in the presence of this internal voice.

THE UNCANNY

Made famous by Freud's 1919 essay 'The Uncanny' but already in use in earlier periods, this has become a widely used term within literary criticism and critical theory. The uncanny refers to a series of disturbances to our certainty, and is most commonly associated with the dead and the ghostly, with *déjà vu*, or with everyday fears and anxieties about repetitions, coincidences, doubles and things not being in quite the right place or time. The uncanny refers not to the strange as such, but instead to the 'strangely familiar' (see Freud 2003 and Royle 2003).

This uncanniness leads to the project of 'making strange what has become familiar'. While not everyone would think of Shakespeare as entirely familiar, nonetheless the strength of Greenblatt's point is clear. There are ways of reading stories, and of reading cultural texts more generally, that will allow us to take account of their unpredictability. Uncomplicated notions of identity give way to a sense of conflict and negotiation within identity. The strange division of Greenblatt's 'own' voice alerts him (and should alert us) to the otherness within any voice, even one as canonical and 'known' as Shakespeare's appears to be.

A story, then, can lead to a critical insight, it can turn out to be something useful for the elaboration of a critical position, and the stories that Greenblatt's work contains are far from incidental to his arguments. In his 1936 essay 'The Storyteller', the German Jewish writer Walter Benjamin comments on 'the nature of every real story', proposing:

> It contains, openly or covertly, something useful. In one case, the usefulness may lie in a moral; in another, in some practical advice; in a third, in a proverb or maxim. In every case the storyteller is a man who has counsel for his readers.

> (Benjamin 2002: 145)

Benjamin contrasts the story to both information and interpretation, complaining that the kinds of narratives that we are given by newspapers tend to come with explanations already embedded in them. This amounts to a closing off of the reader's capacity to interpret for her- or himself. Information presented in this way retains its currency only in the time that it is new, but the story is capable of persisting: 'It preserves and concentrates its energy and is capable of releasing it even after a long time' (Benjamin 2002: 148). Consequently, Benjamin proposes a similar distinction between the historian and the chronicler: the historian must attempt to explain the events with which he deals, whereas the chronicler is able simply to display them, opening a space for the reader's act of interpretation. Ultimately, for Benjamin, the crucial element in story-telling is its reproducibility. The listener to a great story will be attentive because he or she will want to tell the story to others. Memory thus becomes the central feature; the story preserves the memory of a community to the extent that that story lives on in the memories of those who have heard and retold it.

WALTER BENJAMIN (1892–1940)

Walter Benjamin was one of the most extraordinary thinkers of the twentieth century. Combining Marxist ideas with a deep knowledge of both German philosophy and Jewish mysticism, Benjamin's texts engage with subjects as diverse as tragedy, photography, cities, drugs, literature, art, surrealism, modernity and translation. Particularly influential are two essays, 'On the Concept of History' and 'The Work of Art in the Age of Its Technological Reproducibility' (also known as the 'Theses on the Philosophy of History' and 'The Work of Art in the Age of Mechanical Reproduction', but the first set of titles are more accurate translations from the German). The former is of particular interest to historicist critics, and it contains some of Benjamin's most famous statements concerning his version of historical materialism. For Benjamin, our relationship to the past demands not that we should aim to see the past 'as it really was', but instead that we read 'against the grain'. Proposing that what has traditionally been regarded as high culture is always to some extent implicated in a political system based on the oppression of the anonymous workers not recognized in this tradition, Benjamin argues that 'There is no document of civilization which is not at the same time a document of barbarism' (Benjamin 2003: 392). This must be read dialectically, emphasizing the 'at the same time', and Benjamin is not suggesting that artworks are barbaric, but instead that there is a relation between art and barbarism that could, and should, be read by the materialist critic.

As even the brief quotation given here suggests, Benjamin's texts are full of striking images and statements, but these have to be read very carefully in the context of the fuller argument if they are not to be reduced to slogans or catchphrases. Benjamin's style has been the object of much imitation, and his texts often present a series of fragmentary narratives, offering fleeting glimpses of his thinking in place of a more conventional sustained argument, making them very easy to quote. Witty and powerfully polemical, elusive and allusive, these texts are frequently difficult, and the secondary literature on Benjamin's work is enormous. His most well-known works include *Charles Baudelaire* (1973), *Illuminations* (1973), *The Origin of German Tragic Drama* (1977) and *One-Way Street* (1979). If you become seriously interested in Benjamin, however, you should consult the four-volume *Walter Benjamin: Selected Writings* (1996–2003) and *The Arcades Project* (1999).

Greenblatt cites 'The Storyteller' essay in *Marvelous Possessions* (1991: 1), and Benjamin is a recurrent reference point in his work (see Greenblatt 1980: 86; 1992: 147). So, for example, Chapter 2 of *Renaissance Self-Fashioning* is entitled 'The Word of God in the Age of Mechanical Reproduction', which echoes the title of one of Benjamin's most famous essays. Like Benjamin, Greenblatt is interested in the ways in which stories can contain and preserve an 'energy', opening up the culture in which the story originates in an active process of remembering and reproducing, but not seeing that culture as a unified entity. Greenblatt shares the interest not only in the useful truth that the story may contain, but in retelling the story for his own readers. While he does include some interpretation of these stories, there is still a space for them to be taken on by the reader and reinterpreted.

THE HISTORY OF THE ANECDOTE

One of the most famous anecdotes in Greenblatt's work comes at the end of *Renaissance Self-Fashioning*. Greenblatt tells of an eventful flight in which he sits next to a man who, he hoped, was unlikely to disturb his reading (of Clifford Geertz's *The Interpretation of Cultures*, about which more in a moment). But rather than allowing him to read, the man begins to speak, telling Greenblatt that he is on his way to visit his son, who is ill in hospital. The illness has both impaired the son's speech and, says the father, caused him to lose his will to live. Wishing both to restore that will and also to be able to understand the son, the father then asks Greenblatt to mouth some words so that he can practise lip-reading. The sentence that he asks him to say, though soundlessly, is 'I want to die'. Greenblatt is unable to help him, unable, that is, to speak this particular sentence, and a silence falls between them for the remainder of the flight.

What are we to make of this anecdote? Unnerving in itself, there is more to this than simply a sense of the ominous qualities of the sentence. Greenblatt gives a couple of possible reasons for his inability to follow the man's wishes. First, there was the 'paranoid' (Greenblatt's own word) feeling that if he spoke these words then the man would take this as the expression of a death wish and kill him. So, simple fear offers one answer. But there is also something else in his response (or failure to respond) which takes us back to our consideration of stories and their relation to our sense of identity. As Greenblatt explains:

> I felt superstitiously that if I mimed the man's terrible sentence, it would have the force, as it were, of a legal sentence, that the words would stick like a burr upon me. And beyond superstition, I was aware, in a manner more forceful than anything my academic research had brought home to me, of the extent to which my identity and the words I utter coincide, the extent to which I want to form my own sentences or to choose for myself those moments in which I will recite someone else's. To be asked, even by an isolated, needy individual to perform lines that were not my own, that violated my sense of my own desires, was intolerable.
>
> (1980: 256)

Greenblatt fears the performative dimension of the sentence that he is asked to speak. In other words, he fears that the sentence might be a 'death sentence', not so much describing a situation but instead causing something to happen through the act of speaking (on the 'performative' in this sense, see Austin 1976). But more than that, he also experiences the desire to cling to his speech as an expression of his own will. So again we are asked to consider the relation of language to that which is outside it. On the one hand, there is the idea that a linguistic utterance can make something happen in the world (such as the man killing him once he asked to die) and, on the other, there is the effect of speaking on the sense of identity of the one who speaks.

In order to understand the significance of the anecdote for Greenblatt, we need to be aware of its status with regard to the established forms of historiography or of literary history. Part of the objection to the anecdote might be that it seems somehow trivial, that it is too 'small' to be enlisted in the project of writing a history that had any claim to comprehensiveness or objectivity. As a form of story-telling that is not dependent on wider frameworks, seeming to be complete in itself, the anecdote is apparently of little use. But, as we have seen in Benjamin's idea that every real story contains something useful, for some critics the non-coincidence of the anecdote with these larger histories is precisely where its appeal lies.

In an influential essay, 'The History of the Anecdote: Fiction and Fiction', Joel Fineman (who was one of Greenblatt's colleagues at Berkeley until his death, aged 42, in 1989) focuses precisely on the ways in which the anecdote disrupts more conventional historical narratives. Responding, as its subtitle suggests, to Greenblatt's essay 'Fiction and Friction' which appears in *Shakespearean Negotiations*,

Fineman's essay examines the anecdote in both formal and historical terms (although he never actually gets around to discussing Greenblatt's essay directly). Fineman proposes that 'the anecdote determines the destiny of a specifically historiographic integration of event and context'. He continues:

> The anecdote, let us provisionally remark, as the narration of singular event, is the literary form or genre that uniquely refers to the real. This is not as trivial an observation as might at first appear. It reminds us, on the one hand, that the anecdote has something literary about it, for there are, of course, other and non-literary ways to make reference to the real – through direct description, ostention, definition, etc. – that are not anecdotal. On the other hand, it reminds us also that there is something about the anecdote that exceeds its literary status, and this excess is precisely that which gives the anecdote its pointed, referential access to the real.
>
> (Fineman 1991: 67)

The story as anecdote is thus literary and non-literary. Specifically, it offers a reference to the real. This irruption of the real into history is what makes it of such interest to historicist critics. Its sense of being complete unto itself makes it the smallest unit of a historiographical narrative. The anecdote, which we might also call a *petit récit* or *petite histoire* ('little story'), interrupts the historical *grand récit* (or grand narrative), that is, the large and ordered story of historical progression from a determinate beginning to a definite end. As Fineman points out, if we think of new historicism as one of the attempts to break up or break out of the constraint that such an ordered view of history entails, then this is also one of the reasons why new historicism should not be thought of as conforming to Jameson's trans- or ahistorical injunction to 'always historicize' (Fineman 1991: 71) (see Chapter 1, p. 31). Jameson's injunction is wedded to a political position that relies upon a certain view of history as a logical progression. New historicism refuses such historical certainty.

Ultimately, Fineman suggests that 'the anecdote is the literary form that uniquely *lets history happen* by virtue of the way it introduces an opening into the teleological, and therefore timeless, narration of beginning, middle, and end' (1991: 72). Its uniqueness lies in the fact that it does conjure up the features of the grand narrative, the anecdote is not mere description but instead employs formal features such as beginning, middle and end that it shares with other forms of narrative. But at the same time, it does not rely upon any framing narrative or context to make it part of a series or succession. Unlike a historiography that struggles to make all of the parts fit into a coherent whole, the anecdote becomes a 'hole' in that larger narrative (a hole in the whole), neither dependent on it nor subsumable within it. Because the anecdote has been treated as historiographically suspect, and thus not really treated at all in many histories, the emergence of the anecdote punctures the history from which it has been excluded.

There is far more to this essay than the brief account here can contain, and Fineman's argument is of importance not only because it provides one of the most subtle attempts to link new historicist practice at the level of style to its intellectual significance, but also because Gallagher and Greenblatt feel the need to respond to it in *Practicing New Historicism*. They concede much of Fineman's account of the formal characteristics of the anecdote and its function within new historicism, noting their desire to find 'a vehement and cryptic particularity that would make one pause or even stumble on the threshold of history' (Gallagher and Greenblatt 2000: 51). But they also concede that only certain kinds of anecdote seemed to offer the sense of the radical strangeness that they were looking for, only some anecdotes opened up the contingency and unpredictability of history. Anecdotes were used to drive a wedge into the familiar, and the cracks that then appeared were themselves held to be of critical interest. The anecdote, claim Gallagher and Greenblatt:

> could be conceived as a tool with which to rub literary texts against the grain of received notions about their determinants, revealing the fingerprints of the accidental, suppressed, defeated, uncanny, abjected, or exotic – in short, the nonsurviving – even if only fleetingly.

(2000: 52)

The connections both to the work of Benjamin – conjured up in that allusion to reading against the grain – and to Greenblatt's other statements on story and voice are clear. What is proposed is a form of 'counterhistory', that is, a history that is both different from existing histories in its specificity of evidence and in its narrative form, and is also able to take into account what *might have happened* at a given historical moment rather than simply what did. Gallagher and Greenblatt go on to outline the traditions from which their project drew its inspiration, including the historiography of E. P. Thompson and the British radical history movement, and the work of Foucault. One of the things taken from the radical historians, and especially the feminists in that group, was a desire to ask why certain areas of cultural activity were deemed to be historically significant and why others weren't. In accordance with the ideas on culture that we saw in the last chapter, new historicists were reluctant to accept that *any* topic was inherently unsuitable as a subject for historical analysis. One of the problems of the grand narratives of history was their exclusion of much that we could call 'everyday life', and this is one of the most obvious areas in which the anecdote could disrupt those narratives.

THICK DESCRIPTION

As part of his consideration of culture, and as part of his desire to find, within historical narratives and archives, the moments – testified to by stories or anecdotes – that disrupt those narratives and render them unfamiliar, Greenblatt has been influenced by the work of anthropologists, especially Clifford Geertz. In particular, new historicist critics have taken on, following Greenblatt, Geertz's notion of 'thick description'.

What is stressed in Geertz's version of ethnographic anthropology is not so much what ethnography says or what its theoretical dimensions might be, but instead what it is that ethnographers do. As such, it clearly mirrors the emphasis within new historicism on its status as a practice rather than a theory. What ethnographers do, says Geertz (borrowing an idea from British philosopher Gilbert Ryle), is 'thick description'. By this, he means that the work of interpretation is not added to a piece of anthropological data, but is instead an element in all ethnography, since it involves a layering of signification even in its most simple materials. As Geertz puts it:

> Analysis ... is sorting out the structures of signification – what Ryle calls established codes, a somewhat misleading expression, for it makes the enterprise sound too much that of the cipher clerk when it is much more like that of the literary critic – and determining their social ground and import.
>
> (Geertz 1993a: 9)

These structures of signification are in part the product of the fact that the actions of the people being observed are themselves motivated by a sense of what they are trying to achieve by those actions. So any informant who relates a story to the ethnographer will automatically offer a kind of interpretation (an implicit or explicit 'we did this because . . .' or 'we thought it would be a good idea to . . .') even when apparently merely presenting the facts of a situation. Because Geertz believes that the anthropologist should pay attention to symbolic *action*, it doesn't much matter whether we see this action as the product of the mind (so behaviour would indicate a way of thinking) or as a learned form of conduct (emphasizing not the individual will but the social rituals, and so on, that govern behaviour). What matters is what this action means, and, as he proposes, 'Culture is public because meaning is' (1993a: 12). Thick description attempts to take into account the conflicting and shifting structures through which meaning is generated, moving beyond the 'thinness' of a simple enumeration of events and actions or a catalogue of uninterpreted data. Part of what is interesting for our purposes is that Geertz compares the process of ethnographical interpretation to the work of the literary critic. Commenting on the state of anthropology (at least, in 1973), he suggests: 'Meaning, that elusive and ill-defined pseudoentity we were once more than content to leave philosophers and literary critics to fumble with, has now come back into the heart of our discipline' (1993a: 29). So Greenblatt's interest in Geertz partly stems from a recognition that both literary criticism and anthropology share a common concern with meaning and the cultural transactions that shape it. As Gallagher and Greenblatt note, Geertz's work 'made sense of something we were already doing, returning our own professional skills to us as more important, more vital and illuminating, than we had ourselves grasped' (2000: 20).

Geertz sees culture as primarily semiotic, that is, based on the use and interpretation of signs. Culture is thus not a power that can be seen as the cause of events, but rather the context in which those events happen and become meaningful. If all anthropological description is interpretation, then it becomes desirable to take into account the readings that those being observed give of their own actions. Anthropological writings thus tend to be second or third order interpretations (only the actor in the event being capable of a first order interpretation), and are thus what Geertz calls 'fictions'. Glossing this choice of word, he states: 'fictions, in the sense that they are "something made", "something fashioned" – the original meaning of *fictio* – not that they are false, unfactual, or merely "as if" thought experiments' (1993a: 15). In anthropology, these fictions are themselves the things that ethnographers make or do, that is, their primary activity is to write.

What Geertz also stresses, however, is that while anthropology does tend to work with the local and the specific, nonetheless, there is always a relation between the small picture and the bigger picture. But what is this relation? One option is the microcosmic idea, in which, to use his example, a small town in America is taken to somehow encapsulate the nation (or else, that the nation is merely the extrapolation of the features of the small town). There are two problems with this idea. The first is that it's nonsense. The second is that it offers a mistaken view of what the anthropologist studies. As Geertz puts it: 'Anthropologists don't study villages (tribes, towns, neighborhoods . . .); they study *in* villages' (1993a: 22). Instead, 'social actions are comments on more than themselves' (1993a: 23), and the anthropologist takes the specific data and draws from them a significance that goes beyond their local resonances.

What Geertz wants to retain is a sense of dialogue with the people and material under observation. For him, 'The whole point of a semiotic approach to culture is . . . to aid us in gaining access to the conceptual world in which our subjects live so that we can, in some extended sense of the term, converse with them' (1993a: 24). This potentially sets up a tension between theory and the objects of study. Where the tendency of theory is to move towards an abstracted and internally valid structure, claims Geertz, ethnographic study doesn't take ethnography as its starting point in order then to move away from a culture, but instead aims to go deeper into that culture. Rather than employing a transferable theory that allows you to extract some tools from one analysis and turn attention on another object, the ethnographer aims to take on another's argument in order to say more (or say something more accurate) about the same thing. For this reason, says Geertz, there is also a form of writing that is most appropriate to this kind of interpretation: the essay.

THE ESSAY

Certainly, the majority of the influential early work in new historicism can be characterized as essayistic. As Douglas Bruster notes, it was the journal *Representations*, and the collections of essays taken from its pages such as *Representing the English Renaissance* (edited by Greenblatt in 1988) that helped to shape the essay as the dominant form in the interpretation of culture in the 1980s and 1990s (Bruster 2003: 223–4). Similarly, Fineman proposes that 'it is the prosaic and considerable achievement of the New Historicism to have reinvented for our time the essay form invented by Francis Bacon in the Renaissance' (Fineman 1991: 75). Some of Greenblatt's books, such as *Learning to Curse*, are explicitly collections of essays, but even others such as *Shakespearean Negotiations* give the impression that they have been pieced together from a set of discrete parts. A collaborative work such as *Practicing New Historicism* similarly includes two chapters, 1 and 5, that were first published as articles under Greenblatt's own name.

What, then, is the attraction of the essay form? For a scholar of the Renaissance, one of the main temptations to write essays lies in following the example of the great French essayist, Michel de Montaigne, and of his English counterpart, Francis Bacon. Both writers saw their essays as 'attempts' or 'trials', following the French roots of the word '*essai*' or 'essay' in the verb *essayer* (to try or attempt). Bacon and Montaigne sought to communicate something useful to the reader, blending personal experience with material gathered from authorities such as renowned ancient Greek and Roman authors. Yet their choice of the essay form is in part led by a desire to provoke the reader into thinking rather than simply stating, in a magisterial way, what should be thought or done. Montaigne's essays, in particular, are frequently digressive, wandering from the topic announced in the title of his chapter into unexpected and often disconcerting areas. Greenblatt makes many references to Montaigne – his work is mentioned in all of Greenblatt's major books – and the *Essays* are a source of crucial anecdotes and stories around which some of Greenblatt's main essays are built.

There is more to Greenblatt's use of the essay than simply an attraction to the work of a particular influence, however. Essay writing holds a privileged place in critical writing precisely to the extent that it appears to resist some of the more totalizing forms of discourse. As Theodor Adorno puts it, in 'The Essay as Form':

> In the realm of thought it is virtually the essay alone that has successfully raised doubts about the absolute privilege of method. The essay allows for the consciousness of non-identity, without expressing it directly; it is radical

in its non-radicalism, in refraining from any reduction to a principle, in its accentuation of the partial over the total, in its fragmentary character.

(Adorno 1991: 9)

While there is a significant distance between Adorno's critical practice and that of the new historicists, nonetheless his characterization of the essay form clearly echoes the new historicist insistence on a practice that is resistant to the overarching systems of thought that dominate much critical writing. As Adorno goes on to say, the essay suggests a challenge to the idea that truth and history are opposed, in which truth would be historically invariant – what is true is always true, in any given context and for all time – claiming instead that truths are always historically produced:

If truth has in fact a temporal core, then the full historical content becomes an integral moment in it . . . The relationship to experience – and the essay invests experience with as much substance as traditional theory does mere categories – is the relationship to all of history.

(1991: 10)

While traditional critical narratives might claim to say something about everything (or everything about something), the essay by its nature has to offer a more partial view. It makes no claim to state the whole picture, and by doing so it asks the reader to make connections, to see where this piece would fit. This does not serve to reduce its truth content but, instead, echoes the partial nature of our experience of the world. Montaigne is again helpful here. Discussing his own use of examples in constructing his essays, Montaigne addresses the reader directly, proposing that if his examples don't seem to work then his readers should supply their own. For in the end, he is not interested in whether or not his examples are literally true, but in whether or not something can be learned from them:

In the study I am making of our manners and motives, fabulous testimonies – provided they remain possible – can do service as well as true ones. Whether it happened or not, to Peter or John, in Rome or in Paris, it still remains within the compass of what human beings are capable of; it tells me something useful about that. I can see this and profit by it equally in semblance as in reality. There are often different versions of a story: I make use of the one that is rarest and most memorable. There are some authors whose aim is to relate what happened: mine (if I could manage it) would be to relate what can happen.

(Montaigne 1991: 119)

In his interest in story-telling, in his use of anecdotes, and in his favouring of the essay form, Greenblatt is similarly concerned with what it is possible to learn from a narrative, even if that narrative does not relate what we could term a historical event. The texts become an event. His anecdotes are rare and memorable, and rather than giving us a history of humanity or of the totality of a period, they tell us what some human beings are capable of.

SUMMARY

One of the most striking features about new historicism, and Greenblatt's work in particular, has been its style. Greenblatt's work is often organized around stories and anecdotes, and this lends the work a certain flavour, but it also has a more significant role in shaping the kind of history that new historicism presents. Rather than giving an overview of a period or a philosophy of history, new historicist texts tend to focus on counter-histories and on those moments that puncture the grand historical narrative. In part, this emphasis on narrative, story-telling and the anecdote stems from the influence of the anthropologist Clifford Geertz, but it is also to be remarked in the work of a thinker such as Walter Benjamin. It is this concern for rubbing history 'against the grain', both as a stylistic choice and a political principle, that also leads new historicists to favour the essay form in their writing, since the essay is another example of a form that refuses to produce grand narratives.

3

SELF-FASHIONING

Central to an understanding of *Renaissance Self-Fashioning*, Greenblatt's first major book and one which remains one of the key works of new historicism, is the question of identity. As we have already seen, one of Greenblatt's abiding interests is in the possibility of a speaking voice, and the possibility of identifying with that voice so that one can securely say 'I'. In Chapter 2, we saw how Greenblatt relates the voice of the story-teller to a desire to assert identity through narrative, but simultaneously recognizes the extent to which those narratives might also be seen to mark a loss of identity. It is possible to read *Renaissance Self-Fashioning* as an attempt on Greenblatt's part to examine this doubled effect of the narrative or poetic voice in texts of the sixteenth century.

SELF AND IDENTITY

Critical discussion of identity has tended to emphasize two related questions, both of which are central to any project of defining the self. First, there is the debate around whether the self is a natural, 'given' entity – where our characteristics are innate, are what we are born with – or whether it is, instead, socially and culturally constructed through our interactions with the world and with other people. This is often expressed as a distinction between nature and nurture. Second, we may ask whether the focus should be on the individual self or on social and collective identity in terms of categories such as gender, ethnicity, religious or national identity, and so on. As Jonathan Culler has noted (1997: 110–22), the elements of these two questions tend to combine into four main strands of thinking about identity. If we combine the ideas of identity as given and individual, we will see the self as unique, as an inner core or essence which is expressed through our acts and speech. Our sense of self will then remain relatively independent of specific acts or social locations, possessing a kind of constancy. This underlies traditional notions of character, and the value judgements that go with them. So someone will be good or bad not at a given moment but in a fundamental way, and it is easy to see how this carries over into literary notions of hero and villain. Characters do what they do because of who they are, and the villain commits evil acts because he *is* evil. We can see this in Samuel Taylor Coleridge's famous description of the character of Iago in Shakespeare's *Othello* as a 'motiveless malignity', whose destructive acts stem from his essentially evil character. According to this view, Iago's actions are not a response to a situation – he has no motive – but are, instead, the expression of his identity.

The second combination brings together the idea of a given identity and the social. In this view, personal identity is largely determined by factors over which we have no control, such as being born into a particular gender and ethnicity, a specific nationality or place in the social hierarchy, and so on, and our sense of self will be fundamentally related to the social positions that these origins entail. Again, we haven't chosen these features for ourselves, but we identify with the values that attach to them. Thus, in literary terms, we might find this in those stories that present the character whose identity is 'lost' only to be rediscovered by the end of the narrative. Here, an example would be Perdita in Shakespeare's *The Winter's Tale*, a royal child whose nobility shows through despite being raised by shepherds.

Third, we could link the individual and the constructed. Rather than identifying, and identifying with, an essential sense of self, such a view would stress the importance of particular acts in forming an identity. This is the angle taken by existentialism, which, as the name implies, emphasizes the idea that 'existence precedes essence', that is, that we can only discover who we are by examining what we do. As Jean-Paul Sartre (1905–80), the leading figure of French existentialism, puts it:

> man first of all exists, encounters himself, surges up in the world – and defines himself afterwards. If man as the existentialist sees him is not definable, it is because to begin with he is nothing. He will not be anything until later, and then he will be what he makes of himself. ... Man simply is. Not that he is simply what he conceives himself to be, but that he is what he wills, and as he conceives himself after already existing – as he wills to be after that leap towards existence. Man is nothing else but that which he makes of himself.
>
> (Sartre 1989: 28)

Character, then, is not something that we 'have', as an inner core that underpins all our actions, but is rather defined by what we 'do', it is created through our choices and deeds. Sartre's vision of human existence rests on a fundamental atheism, and centrally on the idea that we have not been created to be a particular way by any divine power or God, that is, we have not been given an identity as the expression of a specific purpose. In literature, several of Ernest Hemingway's characters behave according to this principle, particularly Robert Jordan in *For Whom the Bell Tolls*. Even when facing certain death, Jordan wants to die in the 'right' way, and this is shown to be a conscious choice rather than resulting from his 'character'.

Finally, if we combine the social and the constructed, then our identities are formed through the roles that we occupy in the world, and are as much a matter of how we are seen by virtue of those roles as how we see ourselves. The crucial elements of identity thus become occupation (or lack of it), family role (or lack of it), economic or class position, and so on. It is according to such categories that our identities are recognized and judged. Here, an example might be the female character in Joseph Conrad's *Heart of Darkness* who is known only as 'The Intended', and is thus defined primarily through her relationship to Kurtz rather than possessing an independent identity of her own. Her lack of a name means that whenever she appears in the text we are always reminded of the link to him, and her identity remains tied to his even after his death. Other examples might include those texts that include characters for their representative quality – a vicar, a soldier, a prostitute, and so on – where they are not given individuation because their role is to indicate a type of person or to fulfil a particular function in the plot.

Of course, in literary works, the dramatic tension of the text is often created through a conflict between these different ways of thinking about identity. In a novel such as Dickens's *Great Expectations*, there are characters whose view of the world, and of their own place within it, leads them to struggle with the views of others. Thus Pip believes that Miss Havisham is his benefactor in part because he cannot imagine that someone like Magwitch could be. He defines Magwitch according to his sense of the 'criminal'. Likewise, it is inconceivable to him that Estella could be Magwitch's daughter, because he associates her with the social position in which he first encounters her. Conversely, Miss Havisham's identity has become fixed at a particular point in her life, her failed marriage, implying that her sense of self has been determined not by an inner essence but instead through a specific event that happens to her. She then creates Estella's warped sense of the relationship between the sexes, instilling in her a cruelty that is clearly both characteristic and constructed. But by the end of the novel her pride has been broken and she is changed, both in temperament and in physical appearance, suggesting that an identity that has been constructed can be reconstructed. Pip's own identity is subject to change in terms of social position and recognition by others, but it also leads him to feel estranged from Joe and the world in which he grew up. Dickens plays with our sense of the origins of identity by making Pip an orphan, who only knows his parents through what he can read on their tombstones. *Great Expectations* presents these different possibilities, making the reader ask whether character is a matter of innate or inherited features, of childhood and education, of social and economic position, of perception by other people, or of responses to events.

Where, then, does Greenblatt's notion of self-fashioning fit into this thinking on the nature of identity?

SELF-FASHIONING

Let's begin at the beginning. The book opens by stating: 'My subject is *self-fashioning* from More to Shakespeare; my starting point is quite simply that in sixteenth century England there were both selves and a sense that they could be fashioned' (1980: 1). As Greenblatt points out, this is perhaps a little too obvious a statement to be very helpful, since there are always selves (or at least a sense of self) in any period, and identity is always to some extent a matter of deliberate shaping and forming. But there is more to this than meets the eye, since quite what is meant by 'self' and by 'fashion' here needs more precise definition if we are to understand the specifically sixteenth-century dimensions of this claim. Greenblatt raises questions about identity that are of contemporary concern, but he does so in ways that are specific to the sixteenth century.

As the opening paragraph continues, the definition of the self that Greenblatt is employing is given four distinct characteristics: (i) 'a sense of personal order'; (ii) 'a characteristic mode of address to the world'; (iii) 'a structure of bounded desires'; and (iv) 'an element of deliberate shaping in the formation and expression of identity'. There are several aspects to note in this list. The first point focuses on an individual's own sense of self. The second emphasizes how that individual presents her- or himself to the world, and suggests that there is a consistency to this, that it becomes characteristic or idiomatic. In this sense, it is a version of the self that is recognizable to others. Third, the desires of the individual are confined by the individual's sense of limits, or else these desires come into contact with a structure that serves to limit them (and, of course, this may be a combination of the two, since an individual's sense of the bounds of desire may be the internal expression of an external prohibition). This echoes Greenblatt's ideas on culture as restraint that I discussed in Chapter 1. Fourth, not only the formation of identity but also its expression are constructed by an act of will, at least partially chosen rather than wholly given. This fourth point reflects back on the first and second, making clear that Greenblatt is primarily interested in the constructed rather than the given aspects of identity. What this last point also makes clear is that there is always a relationship between one's personal sense of identity and the world in which this identity is expressed and therefore opened up to confirmation or disapprobation. Again, this is reminiscent of the comments in his essay on 'Culture', in which he discusses the ways in which social structures may be demonstrated by informal and non-institutional forms of control. This might be summarized as: self is always in relation to others.

This might seem to be true of every period in history, but Greenblatt notes: 'there is in the early modern period a change in the intellectual, social, psychological, and aesthetic structures that govern the generation of identities' (1980: 1). So Greenblatt is making a claim in this book about a historically specific sense of self and its formation and expression, and his interpretation of the self seeks to take into account the intellectual, the social, the psychological and the aesthetic. Striking a balance between these four factors involves a very specific understanding of culture, as I suggested in Chapter 1.

In the earlier chapters, it was proposed that Greenblatt – in common with other new historicists – sees culture as dynamic, contested and conflictual. Consequently, the definition of the self in his work is similarly a matter of trying to understand how individuals come to terms with, and negotiate between, the competing ideas and possibilities within their culture. Greenblatt sees this process as dialectical. While it is possible to see in the Renaissance a degree of freedom that is generated by new ways of thinking about the individual and the social, at the same time there are also forces which seek to oppose these ways of thinking and, by opposing, end them. There is, he suggests, 'a new stress on the executive power of the will', but there is equally 'the most sustained and relentless assault upon the will' (1980: 1). New social mobility, allowing movements between class and social positions, is accompanied by new constraints on that mobility, and an awareness of alternative forms of social, theological and psychological organization sits alongside concerted attempts to destroy these alternatives. The literary figures that he examines in *Renaissance Self-Fashioning* – Thomas More, William Tyndale, Thomas Wyatt, Edmund Spenser, Christopher Marlowe and William Shakespeare – are drawn into these dialectical processes, and they form their identities through a negotiation with them.

'Fashion' as a verb had a very specific sense in the early modern period. Greenblatt notes that it contained the idea of a literal, physical shaping, but that there was also a more fruitful sense in the terms of his argument. In the Renaissance, 'fashioning may suggest the achievement of a less tangible shape: a distinctive personality, a characteristic address to the world, a consistent mode of perceiving and behaving' (Greenblatt 1980: 2). While much of the discourse on fashioning took as its model the medieval idea of the imitation of Christ, in the early modern secular usage of the term, self-fashioning acquires new meanings:

> it describes the practice of parents and teachers; it is linked to manners or demeanor, particularly that of the elite; it may suggest hypocrisy or deception, an adherence to mere outward ceremony; it suggests representation of one's nature or intention in speech or actions. And with representation we return to literature, or rather we grasp that self-fashioning derives its interest precisely from the fact that it functions without regard for a sharp distinction between

DIALECTICS

Dialectical thinking has a long philosophical tradition. Central to the method of Socrates, dialectics was based on a rational dialogue that proceeded through question and answer towards the truth by a gradual refinement of the dialogue's starting position. So a character in one of Plato's dialogues would be asked to make a clear statement on a given topic, and would then be questioned, leading him to revise his opinion and refine his thinking. Dialectics was thus often associated with Socrates' insistence that a topic should always be broken down into its smallest component parts, often revealing that an initial idea was really a composite of several smaller ideas. As Socrates says in the *Phaedrus*:

> you must know the truth about the subject that you speak or write about; you must be able to isolate it in definition, and having so defined it you must next understand how to divide it into kinds, until you reach the limit of division.
>
> (Plato 1989: 522)

While the definition of dialectics in Plato is generally vague, it is always seen to be positive, and is formalized by Aristotle in the *Topics*. In its simplest form, dialectics is a form of reasoning in which a concept or idea (a *thesis*) is examined in light of its opposite (its *antithesis*). From this it is possible to move to a third position which takes both into account (a *synthesis*). This becomes, in the late medieval and early modern period, part of a method of rhetorical argumentation *in utramque partem* (roughly 'seeing both sides'). A more complex version of this is presented by the German philosopher G. W. F. Hegel (1770–1831). First, a concept is taken to be clear and fixed. Second, contradictions emerge through analysis of the concept that then need to be worked through, and third, a higher concept emerges, which contains both the original concept and its contradictions, allowing for a progression in philosophical knowledge. Hegel also sees this as a feature of world history, in which conflicting forces are resolved in a synthesis, but in history as in philosophy, this is itself merely the first step in the next movement of the dialectic. Thus history, like the progression of philosophical knowledge, is dynamic. This is expressed most famously in his master–slave (or Lordship and Bondage) dialectic (Hegel 1977: 111–19).

literature and social life. It invariably crosses the boundaries between the creation of literary characters, the shaping of one's own identity, the experience of being molded by forces outside one's control, the attempt to fashion other selves. Such boundaries may, to be sure, be strictly observed in criticism, just as we may distinguish between literary and behavioral styles, but in doing so we pay a high price, for we begin to lose a sense of the complex interactions of meaning in a given culture. We wall off literary symbolism from the symbolic structures operative elsewhere, as if art alone were a human creation, as if humans themselves were not, in Clifford Geertz's phrase, cultural artifacts.

(1980: 3)

As we have seen several times already, Greenblatt moves quickly from a description of the material that he is examining to a sense of its critical consequences. Fashioning is of a part with the practices of a culture; its educational modes, its rules of behaviour, its rituals and representations. Literature and the structures of social life are similarly culturally embedded. As in his more general descriptions of culture, Greenblatt proposes that because the phenomena that he is working with do not observe strict divisions between literature and other aspects of the society from which it originates, so the critic cannot observe those boundaries either. It is not that it is impossible to draw the boundaries, simply that if we choose to do so then we must be aware of the critical consequences. But at the end of this description – and largely through the invocation of the anthropological work of Clifford Geertz – we can see him move to a broader claim that goes beyond a particular methodological choice. Human beings themselves, like works of art, are constructions, and these acts of making take place within symbolic structures. So the selves that Greenblatt examines in *Renaissance Self-Fashioning* are formed by, and form, those structures through their interactions with them. Human identity is a product of culture, but humans produce culture.

How, then, should we approach literature in the light of this dialectical sense of production? Greenblatt proposes that 'Literature functions within this system in three interlocking ways: as a manifestation of the concrete behavior of its particular author, as itself the expression of the codes by which behavior is shaped, and as a reflection upon those codes' (1980: 4). This is one of the most important things to note about this book. For Greenblatt, the idea of the 'death of the author' is not one that he takes seriously (see Barthes 1989: 49–55; and Burke 1992).

On the contrary, he invests a great deal of significance in the biography of the author, but we need to think a little more about how that functions. In Chapter 6, I will discuss how Greenblatt tackles the project of writing a biography of Shakespeare in *Will in the World*, so for now just let us note that *Renaissance Self-Fashioning* is predicated on the idea that what he calls the 'concrete' behaviour of the author is crucial in understanding early modern culture. I will show how that works with one of his key examples – Thomas More – in a moment.

It is necessary to be clear about what he sees as the task of the critic in dealing with self-fashioning. Interpretation must address all three aspects of the definition of literature's functions that we have just seen. Greenblatt outlines the risks of not doing so by pointing up the negative aspects of the alternatives. If the critic only looks at the author's biography, then a sense of the larger cultural networks within which the author operates may be lost. If only the social codes that shape behaviour are analysed, then the literary work may get lost in discussion of ideological superstructure (a problem with some forms of Marxist aesthetics in which the urge to reveal what the text does not say leads to a forgetting of what it does say). If only the commentary within a text upon social codes is interpreted, then art can again be seen as detached from a set of concrete relations to both individuals and institutions and loses its connections to social life that Greenblatt is so keen to retain. The solution is, he suggests, to pursue a form of literary criticism that is analogous to Geertzian anthropology:

> A literary criticism that has affinities to this practice must be conscious of its own status as interpretation and intent upon understanding literature as a part of the system of signs that constitutes a given culture; its proper goal, however difficult to realize, is a *poetics of culture*.

(1980: 4–5)

Cultural poetics is seen to be a way to keep in play the intellectual, social, psychological and aesthetic dimensions of self-fashioning.

Having asserted the necessary relation between literature and social life, it is important that we do not understand this as implying that social life is what we are really interested in. Rather than stand as that which is not in need of interpretation or at least as something that doesn't need as much interpretation as literature, Greenblatt stresses that social action is always caught up in signification and interpretation. Because language is a collective construction: 'our interpretive task must be to grasp more sensitively the consequences of this fact by investigating both the social presence to the world of the literary text and the social presence of the world in the literary text' (1980: 5). This neat formulation chimes with Montrose's identification of one of the central premises of new historicism, namely, the 'textuality of history and the historicity of text' that I cited in the 'Why Greeenblatt?' chapter. The insistence on history as textual entails the impossibility of a full historical 'reconstruction'. Texts do not allow you to see *through* them to the world, they are part of the fashioning of that world (see the comments in 1980: 6).

Greenblatt also recognizes that, while it is possible to relate the actions and writings of particular individuals to the symbolic structures operative in a given culture, nonetheless this does not result in a single, unified history of self-fashioning: 'There is no such thing as a single "history of the self" in the sixteenth century, except as the product of our need to reduce the intricacies of complex and creative beings to safe and controllable order' (1980: 8). As we saw in Chapter 2, Greenblatt's project is not to write a traditional history or *grand récit*. Far from producing a grand narrative – and perhaps rather worryingly – Greenblatt proposes that *Renaissance Self-Fashioning* doesn't actually explain Renaissance self-fashioning, but instead outlines conditions common to this process. He gives a list of ten features common to the cases of self-fashioning that he examines. These features include social status, a submission to authority, a relationship between self and other in which the other is seen to be threatening, alien and disorderly, and a complex interaction of self, other and authority that calls into question aspects of all of them. Of the ten points listed, perhaps number 9 is the most generally applicable beyond the specificities of his examples: 'Self-fashioning is always, though not exclusively, in language' (1980: 9). Greenblatt offers the following summary of these common conditions for self-fashioning:

> we may say that self-fashioning occurs at the point of encounter between an authority and an alien, that what is produced in this encounter partakes of both the authority and the alien that is marked for attack, and hence that any achieved identity always contains within itself the signs of its own subversion or loss.

(1980: 9)

The marks of the dialectic can clearly be seen in this insistence on the impurity of the selves fashioned and of the encounters that form them. It is time to see how this works with the example of Thomas More.

PLAYING A PART

If we now turn to one of Greenblatt's examples, we can see how this general sense of self-fashioning works in practice. The first and longest of the chapters in *Renaissance Self-Fashioning* is devoted to Thomas More. As a successful writer, lawyer and politician who is ultimately executed for treason, More is a striking example of the kind of conflict that Greenblatt sees at the heart of culture. Just as importantly, More is a very self-conscious figure, expressing his dilemmas, doubts and beliefs in his published works, and frequently writing *about* doubt and belief itself. More is also a very astute observer of politics, offering a view that is simultaneously that of an 'insider' and that of a sceptical onlooker, as *Utopia* and other works demonstrate. His works contain satire not only of worldly ambition and political power-play, but also of the part that he himself plays in this theatre of political engagement.

Key to Greenblatt's reading of More is the theatrical metaphor. Greenblatt's More is caught between self-fashioning and self-cancellation; he is able to perform with great success in the spectacle of royal power, but at the same time he is driven by a desire to escape from the role that he has created for himself. More's own tastes are far removed from the luxurious display and casual brutality of a world in which the King proved his power through excessive wealth and the capacity to decide who should live and who should die. Pondering why a man like More would have become involved in this political world in the first place, Greenblatt asks:

> why should men submit to fantasies that will not nourish or sustain them? In part, More's answer is *power*, whose quintessential sign is the ability to impose one's fictions upon the world: the more outrageous the fiction, the more impressive the manifestation of power. ... The point is not that anyone is deceived by the charade, but that everyone is forced either to participate in it or to watch it silently.
>
> (1980: 13)

This is a more complex understanding of politics than we are often led to accept. Rather than the purpose of political display being to

THOMAS MORE AND *UTOPIA*

Thomas More (1478?–1535) is one of the most fascinating figures of the early modern period. Noted as the foremost humanist scholar in England, he wrote a series of influential works on a wide range of topics including theology and history, but his most famous work was the *Utopia*. More trained as a lawyer, and also had a remarkable political career, culminating in his becoming Lord Chancellor of England under Henry VIII, a role from which he was to resign when he found himself unable to take an oath that would recognize Henry as the Supreme Head of the Church in England. As a fervent Catholic who had been active in the pursuit and punishment of heretics, More was unable to reconcile himself to the break with Papal authority. Initially allowed to retire from public life, More was eventually imprisoned and found guilty of treason after perjured evidence was given against him. He was executed in 1535, and declared a Saint by the Catholic Church in 1935.

More's *Utopia* (1516) remains one of the most important works of political philosophy ever written. Originally published in Latin, it was translated into English in 1556. Inspired by Greek sources such as Plato's *Republic*, More's *Utopia* is a discourse on the best state of a commonwealth. But the title contains a play on words (as do many of the names in the book) that unsettles any attempt to pin down its true meaning. The word 'utopia' is not one that existed in Greek, and the 'u-' prefix derives either from 'ou' or 'eu' in Greek. If it is 'eu-topia' then it means 'perfect place', but if it is instead 'ou-topia' then it means 'no place'. This problem – that the island described in the book is either perfect, or that it doesn't exist, or that the perfect place cannot exist – is only the first of many that the text presents to its readers. Similarly, the names in the text provide learned jokes to undermine the apparently serious social and political content. The man who describes the island is called 'Hythloday', which in Greek means 'expert in nonsense'. There is a river on the island called 'Anyder', meaning 'waterless', and a King called 'Ademos', literally 'without a people'. Much of the comedy derives from an inversion of the values of More's own culture. Gold and fine clothes, for example, are worn only by slaves. Like any satire, the fictional elements are close enough to the truth to be disturbing even as they provoke humour. Few would want to live in Utopia, even if it existed, but it has prompted thought on what the ideal commonwealth *would* look like since its first publication.

deceive, here there is no effective deceit. Instead, power lies in the ability to persuade people to behave according to certain rules and principles even though and precisely to the extent that they *do not* believe in them. More's 'is a world in which everyone is profoundly committed to upholding conventions in which no one believes; somehow belief has ceased to be necessary' (1980: 14). Beneath the theatricality of the spectacle, there is nothing at all, but this doesn't stop the spectacle of power from being effective. While this is plausibly enough presented as More's own view on the operations of power, we can see here the influence of Foucault's proposition that power is not a matter of its imposition from above but instead depends on the complicity of all those in a given culture who adopt a role within a power structure (see pp. 20–2 above).

While recognizing More's ultimate failure to reconcile himself to the structures of power in his culture, nonetheless Greenblatt is keen to stress More's success at negotiating the complexities of the system. The absurdity of the world that he inhabits is registered in his fondness for the idea of theatricality. To see the world as theatre is to admit its fictive qualities while at the same time suspending disbelief long enough to reveal the powerfully seductive nature of those fictions. Whatever critical distance More felt from his world, still he played a part within it: 'if the theatrical metaphor expresses his inner sense of alienation and his observation of the behavior of the great, it also expresses his own mode of engagement in society' (1980: 29). More's self-fashioning thus combines the main characteristics that Greenblatt identifies in his introduction. There is a sense of personal order (in the distance that More can see between himself and the world); there is a characteristic mode of address (in More's role-playing); there are bounded desires (More's desire to withdraw from public life is limited by his recognition of the necessity of engagement); and there is evidence of a deliberate shaping of identity (More's self-consciousness about the roles that he plays and the stages on which this playing takes place). More's texts also encapsulate the sense of literature that Greenblatt outlines: they express More's behaviour, they reveal the codes of his society that shape and limit that behaviour, and they comment upon those codes.

This is most clearly seen in Greenblatt's reading of *Utopia*. Drawing attention to the text's dialectical aspects, Greenblatt emphasizes the divisions within the book: between Books 1 and 2; between the 'real' More and the character of Morus, his fictional counterpart; between

Morus and Hythloday; between the text's realist elements and the deliberate undercutting of realism. This is made particularly acute in a debate
that occurs in Book 1. Hythloday complains that there is no room in
a king's court for one who would tell the truth and give good counsel
without self-interest. Morus responds, granting that academic philosophy
may not be appropriate in every context, but insisting that:

> There is another philosophy, better suited for the political arena, that takes its
> cue, adapts itself to the drama in hand, and acts its part neatly and appropriately.
> This is the philosophy for you to use. . . . Wouldn't it be better to take a silent
> role than to say something wholly inappropriate, and thus turn the play into
> a tragicomedy? You pervert the play and ruin it when you add irrelevant
> speeches, even if they are better than the play itself. So go through with the
> drama in hand as best you can, and don't spoil it all just because you happen
> to think of another one that would be better.

(More 1989: 35–6)

Who is speaking here, Morus or More? It is tempting to see this as an
accurate statement on More's own political life. Even when he found
himself unable to continue to play his political role, he chose resignation
and public silence rather than speak out against Henry. The reference
to tragicomedy encapsulates both More's sense of the danger of inter-
fering with the games of kings and his sense of their inherent absurdity.
There is still the recognition that there might be some better way of
conducting political life in his comments on 'irrelevant speeches', but
he counsels against giving voice to it.

The rest of *Utopia* does present that alternative, however, and it is
here that we must recognize that Morus is precisely not More, or at
least is only one aspect of More. One of the key features of Utopia,
suggests Greenblatt, is the relentless reduction of individuality and of
private property, including the idea of self-possession. The Utopians
all dress the same, live in identical houses, eat together, work together
and live in cities that have no local characteristics to distinguish them.
Other than the King, none of the citizens are ever named. Utopia thus
embodies the self-cancellation that shadows More's self-fashioning, but
it does so in a playful manner that cannot be taken as entirely serious
self-criticism (1980: 54). The competing ideas in *Utopia* cannot be
rendered coherent, but neither can they be isolated from each other.

For Greenblatt, one aspect of the text makes this very clear. In the description of Utopia in Book 2, More is absent, but 'his very absence is paradoxically a deep expression of his sense of himself, for . . . his self-fashioning rests upon his perception of all that it excludes, all that lies in perpetual darkness, all that is known only as absence' (1980: 58). The different personae in *Utopia* are aspects of More's identity – he is as much Hythloday, the one who wishes to speak truth to power, as Morus, the cautious statesman – and thus the perception of a threateningly alien otherness that Greenblatt notes as constitutive of self-fashioning lies within More, not outside him.

The reading of More that Greenblatt produces, then, rests on a conception of the self that is focused on the cultural negotiation necessary to fashion an identity. Rather than having an essential sense of personal identity that is unified and given, More is seen to be involved in fluid and complex processes that involve the production and reproduction of this selfhood. There is an overwhelming sense of conflict, and Greenblatt's insistence that More is forced to cancel senses of self as well as fashion them reveals the struggle at the heart of attaining and retaining an identity. Greenblatt's dialectical mode of argumentation – seeing both sides, and taking into account not only the way that culture impacts on individuals but also the ways in which those individuals shape culture – mirrors the dialectical processes that he analyses. Literature does not give us access to 'Thomas More', a singular, fixed individual, but instead shows that More's identity was produced precisely as a failed compromise between incompatible aspects of the self.

When he concludes the book, Greenblatt suggests that such a sense of conflict and failed compromise characterizes all of the figures that he reads here. As he puts it:

Whenever I focused sharply upon a moment of apparently autonomous self-fashioning, I found not an epiphany of identity freely chosen but a cultural artifact. If there remained traces of free choice, the choice was among possibilities whose range was strictly delineated by the social and ideological system in force.

(1980: 256)

Identity is culturally constructed, so Greenblatt would not accept the idea of an innate natural definition of the self, and even the freedom to choose that I suggested was central to existentialist conceptions of the self, is rejected in the proposal that ultimately social and ideological forces prevail over individual desires. Yet the fiction of autonomous selfhood remains. Greenblatt recognizes that the sense that we shape our own identities may be an illusion. Nonetheless, it is an illusion in which we would like to believe.

SUMMARY

This chapter examines Greenblatt's first major book, *Renaissance Self-Fashioning*, which is often seen to be the earliest example of new historicism. Discussion is focused on the negotiation of identity, and on the key term of his title, self-fashioning. In trying to define the self, Greenblatt examines the interplay between individual freedom and expression, and the limits that are imposed by the social structures that an individual encounters. This leads to a discussion of the first and longest chapter in the book, devoted largely to Thomas More's *Utopia*, in which Greenblatt stresses the significance of role-playing and theatricality to the formation of identity. This sense of the world as theatre allows people to recognize the extent to which their senses of self are the results of role-playing, and this allows for a critical distance to open up between the individual and the world. Negotiation with the world allows for the emergence of incompatible aspects of the self, and incompatible desires. Identity is ultimately a cultural construction, and while the fiction that individuals have the power to shape their own identities is revealed to be an illusion, it is an illusion in which people continue to believe.

THE CIRCULATION OF SOCIAL ENERGY

THE WILL TO BE HEARD

Shakespearean Negotiations begins with a now-famous statement, perhaps the most famous of all new historicist pronouncements, which is itself all about beginnings: 'I began with the desire to speak with the dead.' Greenblatt continues:

> This desire is a familiar, if unvoiced, motive in literary studies, a motive organized, professionalized, buried beneath thick layers of bureaucratic decorum: literature professors are salaried, middle-class shamans. If I never believed that the dead could hear me, and if I knew that the dead could not speak, I was nonetheless certain that I could re-create a conversation with them. Even when I came to understand that in my most intense moments of straining to listen all I could hear was my own voice, even then I did not abandon my desire. It was true that I could hear only my own voice, but my own voice was the voice of the dead, for the dead had contrived to leave textual traces of themselves, and those traces make themselves heard in the voices of the living. Many of the traces have little resonance, though every one, even the most trivial or tedious, contains some fragment of lost life; others seem uncannily full of the will to be heard. It is paradoxical, of course, to seek the living will of the dead in fictions, in places where there was no live bodily being to begin with. But those who love literature tend to find more intensity in simulations – in the formal, self-conscious miming of life – than in any of the other textual

traces left by the dead, for simulations are undertaken in full awareness of the absence of the life they contrive to represent, and hence they may skillfully anticipate and compensate for the vanishing of the actual life that has empowered them. Conventional in my tastes, I found the most satisfying intensity of all in Shakespeare.

(1990: 1)

As in *Renaissance Self-Fashioning*, there is a link here between the author, the text and the critic, and it is one that is founded upon a certain conception of voice. Starting out from a desire to hear and to speak to the dead, Greenblatt realizes that it is only through the voices of the living that this dead speech can appear. These dead voices have a 'resonance', and this becomes another of his key concepts (which will be discussed in Chapter 5). The idea of a conversation, even an impossible one – one that could never quite capture the living presence of the writer and in which it would never be possible for that writer to hear the critic – opens up this question of the relationship to the past in a compelling way. What the textual traces that we call literature register is the 'will' of the author, and this takes on a peculiar, uncanny power in fiction. For those who love literature, the fictional representation of life can feel more 'lively', more intense, than other kinds of textual trace such as historical documents or supposedly factual accounts, and may even come to feel more 'real' in some important, lived sense than what is often called 'real life'. Such intensity lies behind, for instance, the way in which readers may identify themselves with a particular character from a literary work.

For Greenblatt, this power is another aspect of cultural, and not simply personal, production. What really interests Greenblatt about Shakespeare, then, is the way in which the intensity of his works, their sense of life, relates to the society in which he lived and wrote. Yet this intensity is not contained by that society, in that it is felt by readers for whom any connection to that society is at best strained. Calling Shakespeare a 'total artist', he describes early modern culture as a 'totalizing society', by which he means a society that claims a link between the human, the natural and the cosmic (sometimes referred to as the 'great chain of being'), and that simultaneously grants a privileged place within this structure to a ruling elite. Having set up these two poles of interest, Greenblatt quickly abandons them. His work on self-fashioning, he suggests, led him to revise the idea of the total artist, if by that we wished to understand a unified and complete individuality. As I suggested in the previous chapter, self-fashioning is revealed to be a process deeply riven by conflict and ultimately failing in its desire to assert a stable sense of personal identity. Equally, early modern society, and in particular its power structures, similarly fails to render up a sense of control and completion and is thus not in any plausible way totalized. Any monolithic idea of power, especially of state power, must be seen to rest on tensions that cannot be thought or wished away. The fact that there is a desire to totalize reveals precisely that this form of society is not in place.

WORLD PICTURES

In order to understand this more fully, it is helpful to contrast Greenblatt's ideas here with those of an earlier critic of the early modern period. The English critic E. M. W. Tillyard famously wrote about what he called the 'Elizabethan World Picture' in 1943. Reading a series of official documents from the Elizabethan period alongside literary works such as Shakespeare's plays, Tillyard drew out what he saw as the dominant views held within Elizabethan society about order, religion, politics, and so on. In this respect, Tillyard was a forerunner of later historicist critics such as Greenblatt. But Tillyard's reading of these texts led him to posit a vision of the period in which there was a definite sense of order, harmony and orthodoxy. This view is obviously very unlike that of the new historicists and cultural materialists, and Tillyard's work has often been explicitly criticized by them. Central to their disagreement is the sense that Tillyard tends to read the documents of the period at face value, so, if a series of proclamations assert the necessity of obedience to the sovereign, then this shows that such obedience is part of the widely held beliefs of the society, and thus that most people are obedient. Tillyard's sense of the Elizabethan period is thus a totalized one, in that he sees an accord between official policy and people's behaviour. As Dollimore puts it: 'The error, from a materialist perspective, is falsely to unify history and social process in the name of "the collective mind of the people"' (Dollimore and Sinfield 1994: 5; see also Grady 1994: Chapter 4). What later historicists would suggest is that if the need for obedience has to be repeatedly stressed, it is precisely because people are *not* being obedient. Official documents become evidence of the failure of behaviour to match up with policy. Positive and negative readings of the same material are possible, depending on the critic's broader vision of the culture that produces that material. This is another example of the way in which new historicists tend to read against the grain.

As Greenblatt notes, having disposed of the ideas of total artist and totalizing society, it might seem desirable simply to return to the text 'in itself'. So the possibility of formalism is always there. But he proposes something else, that is, to read Shakespeare's canonical texts against other texts that are at the 'borders' or 'margins' of the canon, offering a reading of the period's literary production that is more fragmentary than complete. One of the functions of this practice, as opposed to the author-based readings to be found in *Renaissance Self-Fashioning*, is to convey a sense of the collective production of literary culture. As I have already suggested in earlier chapters, for a historicist such as Greenblatt, no text appears in the world simply through the efforts of a single person, and no text is entirely disconnected from the world in which it makes its appearance. As such, of course, the fragmentary mode of reading exemplified in *Shakespearean Negotiations* stands as another deliberate avoidance of the grand narrative approach to history. Shakespeare thus is and is not representative of early modern culture. His works offer modern readers a way into thinking about early modern culture, and have become a privileged site for such readings, but what those readings pursue is not 'Shakespeare's' works as the product of a privileged individual but, instead, as a series of cultural negotiations. For Greenblatt, there is an explicitly political aspect to this sense of collective production:

> In literary criticism Renaissance artists function like Renaissance monarchs: at some level we know perfectly well that the power of the prince is largely a collective invention, the symbolic embodiment of the desire, pleasure, and violence of thousands of subjects, the instrumental expression of complex networks of dependency and fear, the agent rather than the maker of social will. Yet we can scarcely write of prince or poet without accepting the fiction that power directly emanates from him and that society draws upon this power.
>
> (1990: 4)

This collective dimension is particularly acute in the case of theatrical texts, which are always animated by a sense of collaboration in production and a collective audience. As part of social practice, textual traces circulate within an economy of production and consumption, and their capacity to generate interest and pleasure derives from their place within that economy.

SOCIAL ENERGY

What Greenblatt calls 'social energy' is the force that a text or artefact takes on, its capacity to have an effect on the mind of the hearer or reader. Derived by Greenblatt from the rhetorical term *energia*, this form of energy

> is manifested in the capacity of certain verbal, aural, and visual traces to produce, shape, and organize collective physical and mental experiences . . . it is associated with repeatable forms of pleasure and interest, with the capacity to arouse disquiet, pain, fear, the beating of the heart, pity, laughter, tension, relief, wonder.

(1990: 6)

Energia refers to those figures of speech that make an image vivid in the mind of the listener, and in Aristotle's *Rhetoric* it is described as bringing something 'before your eyes', that is, making the hearer see things (Aristotle 1995: 2252). In terms of artworks, the interest in this for Greenblatt lies especially in those works (or those moments within works) which seem to retain the power to move someone, to laughter or tears, anger or anxiety, beyond the confines of a given cultural moment, allowing the texts to be effective in other places or times. For Greenblatt this power comes not from the hand of the artist but, instead, from a series of negotiations, exchanges and movements. How, then, does this work?

Greenblatt suggests that the central issue is one of exchange. Writers and theatrical companies take objects, ideas, figures of speech and narratives that are already in existence and transfer them to the script and the stage. Such exchanges could take various forms in the early modern period, but include *appropriation* (in which objects are freely taken from the public domain, including language, and nothing need be given in return), *purchase* (in which objects are bought, such as costumes, properties and books used as sources, and the writer is paid), and *symbolic acquisition* (generally, the representation of social practices and energies, where the trade-off would be the celebration or denigration of that which is represented). In each case, a relationship between the aesthetic practices of the theatre and other social practices is established. This relationship is seen to be dynamic, in which the theatre not only borrows or buys objects from the wider culture, but in doing so also allows for a reconception of the objects or practices presented. Thus the theatrical performance might draw force from presenting a social ritual, such as the investiture of a king, but the ritual might additionally be held up for scrutiny, mockery or awe. Theatrical performance thus opens up a critical distance between the objects and practices that it presents and the audience's response. Just as a sense of the theatricality of everyday life, and particularly political life, allowed Thomas More to retain a sceptical fascination for the mechanics of power in *Renaissance Self-Fashioning*, so the literal staging of social practices allows the theatrical dimension of their original 'performance' in everyday life to be seen and judged.

In interpreting theatrical practice, then, Greenblatt suggests a series of principles that should govern the critic's response:

1   There can be no appeals to genius as the sole origin of the energies of great art.

2   There can be no motiveless creation.

3   There can be no transcendent or timeless or unchanging representation.

4   There can be no autonomous artifacts.

5   There can be no expression without an origin and an object, a *from* and a *for*.

6   There can be no art without social energy.

7   There can be no spontaneous generation of social energy.

(1990: 12)

What is again stressed here is the collective nature of aesthetic production. No object and no individual stands outside of the dynamic and social system of exchange. Artistic practices occupy a specific place within this system, and rules are generated both by the theatrical companies and by other authorities that govern how it functions. The theatre is differentiated from other aspects of a culture, but it is always in relation to them, and this relation is fluid and open to renegotiation.

Ultimately, suggests Greenblatt, while the theatre might not have an obvious use value – being marked out as a domain in which pleasure can be perceived as non-practical, despite the uses to which pleasure may itself be put – the boundaries that mark it off from other social practices are permeable. Theatrical practices which partake of the exchange of social energy are part of a system that is 'partial, fragmentary, conflictual; elements were crossed, torn apart, recombined, set against each other; particular social practices were magnified by the stage, others diminished, exalted, evacuated' (1990: 19). While the focus of his reading of early modern culture may have shifted, Greenblatt's sense of that culture remains the same: culture is a space of conflict and competition. A critical practice that attempts to take account of this must have a similar structure, and it is tempting to read this description of theatrical practice as equally applicable to Greenblatt's method. As I will show, his readings of early modern texts are also partial and fragmentary, and rely on the recombination of elements in a way that magnifies certain aspects of the plays and diminishes or even evacuates others.

SUBVERSION AND CONTAINMENT

The most celebrated and controversial chapter in *Shakespearean Negotiations* is the essay 'Invisible Bullets', in which Greenblatt presents a reading of Shakespeare's *Henry IV* plays and *Henry V*. Appearing in three different publications prior to inclusion in his own book, this essay generated considerable debate primarily because of its presentation of a key argument which centres on 'subversion and containment'.

The essay begins by considering the work of Thomas Harriot, who wrote one of the earliest accounts of the English colonies in America, *A Brief and True Report of the New Found Land of Virginia* (1588). Greenblatt focuses on the section in Harriot's narrative in which he discusses the imposition of the Christian religion on the Algonquian Indians. Paradoxically, Harriot's text mobilizes one of the criticisms of organized religion – that it is merely imposed by men in authority on the vulnerable and credulous – in order to show how the colonial mission carries out its officially sanctioned work of converting the native Americans, leading them into belief in, and obedience to, the Christian God and the institutions and men who represent that religion. In particular, Harriot notes how the colonizers use products of human ingenuity and invention such as telescopes, clocks, guns and books, to demonstrate the superiority of their religion over the apparently more 'primitive' (because less technological) faith of the indigenous peoples. In other words, human powers of invention are used to prove the power of God – or at least, one particular God. The paradox in this is obvious. If institutionalized Christian religion is criticized within Europe as the invention of men, then for Christians to use human inventions to assert the strength of their religion only adds credence to the criticism. This should lead to a subversion of religion, or at least to a more profound scepticism. But in Harriot's account, the colonizing power draws upon subversive elements in order to strengthen itself. Subversion becomes the foundation of a power that is reinforced precisely through its capacity to contain that subversion (1990: 30). The imposition of religion, as it is portrayed at least in Harriot's text, is read by Greenblatt as a kind of analogue or allegory of the wider functioning of political power, especially in a colonial context. Power and subversion are not opposed in any simple fashion; they are, instead, intricately related and interdependent. There is a clear echo here of the argument about power in Greenblatt's reading of Thomas More. The fact that the spectacle of power produces illusions in which no one believes does not mean that people do not participate in these fictions. Again, scepticism is no barrier to obedience.

Intriguingly, when Greenblatt comes to define what he understands by 'subversive', he proposes that what modern readers find subversive in early modern culture are precisely ideas that are *not* subversive in the modern period. That is, these ideas have now come to seem true or real but because they emerged in early modern culture, they were often perceived as a threat. Greenblatt's argument here is similar to that proposed by Raymond Williams, who suggests that a culture could be divided into dominant, residual and emergent elements (see Williams 1989: Chapter 8). At any given moment there are new ideas and practices emerging that will become part of the dominant element of culture. At the same time, there are ideas that are still present in a culture but which are no longer part of the mainstream (hence, residual). An example of this process of emergence might be the idea that the Sun, rather than the Earth, is the centre of the solar system. This idea is readily accepted in modern culture, but was resisted in the sixteenth and seventeenth centuries by the Roman Catholic Church, and was one of the ideas that led to the appearance of the astronomer and scientist Galileo Galilei (1564–1642) before the Inquisition in 1616. That there were attempts to control, deny or destroy subversive forces, ideas or impulses in the Renaissance period demonstrates their subversive nature *then*, but they pose no threat to us. Equally, that which modern readers identify as 'orthodox' in early modern culture would seem largely alien to them, but not subversive. Such ideas are not seen to be threatening. As such, these ideas are 'contained' in the same way that Renaissance culture contained its subversive elements. Following on from this insight, Greenblatt ends the opening section of this essay with the claim, parodying Kafka, that 'There is subversion, no end of subversion, only not for us' (1990: 39).

SHAKESPEARE AND SUBVERSION

The structure of this argument becomes clearer when he turns to Shakespeare's plays. Greenblatt begins by stating that 'Shakespeare's plays are centrally, repeatedly concerned with the production and containment of subversion and disorder . . . above all in the plays that meditate on the consolidation of state power' (1990: 40). Not unique in doing so, nonetheless Shakespeare's plays present the social energies circulating between the centres and margins of his culture in a particularly concentrated and powerful manner, and, for Greenblatt, Shakespeare does not represent these exchanges so much as appropriate them, in the sense indicated above. Borrowing freely from his culture, the writer is able to draw on existing forces to provoke interest, pleasure, pain or disquiet, or a range of other responses. So it is not simply a case of using these elements as source material, but instead they are employed in order to intensify the dramatic effect of the play on the audience.

This interpretation is focused on the figure of Prince Hal in *1 Henry IV*. As Hal accumulates authority, foreshadowing his status as the idealized figure of an English King in *Henry V*, there emerges not merely a sense of the solidity of his character, but also the interplay of this character's subversion and the containment of that subversion. Caught between his father's disappointment and the hopes of his friends, Hal will 'falsify' both, that is, he will fail to live down or up to their expectations. As he moves towards a 'redemption' in *2 Henry IV* and *Henry V*, Hal's involvement with the world of the taverns is seen not so much as his subversion of his father's authority, or of his future role as king, but instead as a facet of his apprenticeship, as a preparation for this later rule. Hal's role-playing, in which he takes on many parts, including 'himself', is read as a kind of theatrical improvisation, not a million miles from that of More in *Renaissance Self-Fashioning* (see 1990: 52, where Hal's 'self-fashioning' is explicitly named). As a form of improvisation, Hal's involvement with Falstaff and the other 'lower' characters becomes purposeful. His apparent idleness and dissolution is turned into a kind of training for the improvisation that will be necessary in his future role.

In *2 Henry IV*, Warwick conveys this sense of Hal's project to his father, but the description is hardly reassuring:

> The Prince but studies his companions
> Like a strange tongue, wherein, to gain the language,
> 'Tis needful that the most immodest word
> Be look'd upon and learnt, which once attain'd,
> Your Highness knows, comes to no further use
> But to be known and hated. So, like gross terms,
> The Prince will in the perfectness of time
> Cast off his followers, and their memory
> Shall as a pattern or a measure live,
> By which his Grace must mete the lives of other,
> Turning past evils to advantages.

(4.4.67–78)

The Prince does indeed cast off his followers. At the close of the second play, the betrayal of Falstaff acts to cancel the 'betrayal' of Hal's royal destiny that his 'past evils' seemed to connote. But part of the apparent harshness of this ending comes from a sense that it has been calculated, as if it had been intended all along, as if the subversive elements that Falstaff embodies were produced only to be contained.

When we reach *Henry V*, the conflict between the charismatic authority of the new king and the sense of royal power as a deceptive and theatrical display based on betrayal remains evident. As Greenblatt comments, the mark of true authority in the play 'is precisely the ability to betray one's friends without stain [on one's character]' (1990: 58). The unease that we experience in watching Henry order the execution of Bardolph or the killing of the French prisoners mixes uneasily with the celebratory aspects of the victory at Agincourt or the wooing of the French princess. It is precisely this ambiguous portrayal of the King, however, that provokes the audience's interest, and its power to intrigue and entertain is heightened rather than lessened by its failure to provide an uncomplicated celebration of English kingship. In a way that is specific to Elizabethan culture, audiences must imaginatively identify with the royal authority depicted not only on the stage but in the political sphere, accepting the legitimacy of that authority in part because of the doubts that it raises. The plays contain the subversive thoughts that they provoke through their ability to prompt this identification.

It is in this vision of political complicity and containment that critics have fastened on a potential problem with the new historicist enterprise. Reading this subversion and containment argument as an emblem of the politics of Greenblatt's work more generally, it has been objected that this view dampens and cancels any real resistance to power (see Jonathan Gil Harris's survey of these arguments in Herman 2004: Chapter 6). Such critics point not only to the argument presented in 'Invisible Bullets' but also to the suggestion at the end of *Renaissance Self-Fashioning* that, as his work on that book progressed, 'the human subject itself began to seem remarkably unfree, the ideological product of the relations of power in a particular society' (1980: 256). Greenblatt has responded to this charge, conceding the plausibility of a claim that if every site of resistance is ultimately co-opted by power then this is an overly bleak assessment. He counters that he has never said that all instances of resistance are contained: 'Some are, some aren't' (1992: 165). This is perhaps a little too brief as a response to satisfy his critics, however, and it doesn't really explain why he chooses not to write about successful resistance.

SHAKESPEARE AND THE EXORCISTS

In the chapter of *Shakespearean Negotiations* entitled 'Shakespeare and the Exorcists', Greenblatt turns to *King Lear*. Characteristically, in tackling one of the most well known and widely discussed of Shakespeare's tragedies, he begins by addressing the perhaps unexpected topic of exorcism. Drawing together the play with Samuel Harsnett's 1603 *A Declaration of Egregious Popish Impostures* – a text that has long been thought of as a source for Shakespeare's play – Greenblatt suggests that: 'The relation between these two texts enables us to glimpse with unusual clarity and precision the institutional negotiation and exchange of social energy' (1990: 94). Countering the 'inert' tradition of source studies that simply tell readers what Shakespeare has 'borrowed' from other material, Greenblatt is interested in seeing the extent to which there may be a more complex interaction between these two texts, asking what Harsnett's text might have taken from the theatre. Does this interaction allow us to trace a 'larger cultural text' (1990: 95) that is produced through this exchange?

Central to both texts is a negotiation of cultural value and, in particular, the status of the sacred within early modern culture. The category of the sacred is one that crosses the boundaries between the religious and the secular, since early modern monarchy always claimed a degree of sacredness, and the monarch was often regarded as 'God's lieutenant'. This is sometimes thought of as the so-called divine right of kings, in which religious obedience and obedience to the state are combined. This is exemplified and reinforced in a country in which the monarch is also the Supreme Head of the Church in England, and the Reformation recasting of religion in England made ever more apparent the link between religious and secular power. Rethinking the sacred thus involves rethinking the relation between the individual, the state and God. Where exorcism becomes of interest is primarily in its enactment as a public ritual; when an exorcism is performed in this period it is done so in front of a large crowd, and takes on an inevitably theatrical dimension. There is always the suspicion, however, that such exorcisms were merely performances, and Harsnett in this text is sceptical of the legitimacy of claims to have cured possession or to have cast out devils, especially those of Catholics (hence the reference to 'Popish' in his title). For Harsnett, exorcism is a form of fraud.

What lay at the root of Harsnett's objections to exorcism was not the validity of the ritual itself, however, but the effect that it had upon the spectators. Greenblatt identifies the power of exorcism with an experience of the uncanny (discussed above, see pp. 35–6). While the invocation of devils and possession might be thoroughly strange, those possessed tended to be neighbours and the rituals of exorcism took place in familiar surroundings (1990: 103). This strange familiarity appears in the testimony of the witnesses that Greenblatt cites. But it also leads us back to theatricality. Harsnett's account of exorcism stresses the fact that it is fraudulent, an illusion that depends upon tricks, stage management, the recital of a script, and the belief (or 'suspension of disbelief') of the audience. Harsnett's text is an attempt to break the theatrical spell, to reveal the smoke and mirrors that lie behind the performance of this religious ritual. As Greenblatt comments:

> To glimpse the designing clerical playwright behind the performance is to
> transform terrifying supernatural events into a human strategy. One may then
> glimpse the specific material and symbolic interests served by this particular
> strategy, above all by its clever disguising of the fact that it is a strategy.
>
> (1000: 107)

Just as Greenblatt's argument in the discussion of the colonial encounter
between Christian and non-Christian in Harriot's text centres on the
transactions between the sacred and the secular – where human inventions were used to prove the power of the Christian God – so here
he looks at the process in reverse: the supernatural becomes the human
in order to empty it of its power. At stake in both of these processes
is the effect on the mind of the spectator. In Harriot, fear is deliberately
provoked by the colonists to control the Native American spectators
whom they encounter; in Harsnett, fear is deliberately reduced in
order to release the English spectators from the power of religious
ritual. In both cases, what is presented is not a vision of power as the
physical domination of a weak force by a stronger one, it is instead a
matter of force lying in the employment of a quasi-theatrical presentation
that works upon the minds of those who watch. Power is invested in
performance, but there is also a power in being able to show that
a spectacle is nothing more than a performance. As Greenblatt
says, 'Performance kills belief; or rather acknowledging theatricality
kills the credibility of the supernatural' (1990: 109).

These negotiations between the secular and the sacred, between the
material world of the theatre and the spiritual realm of religion, can
be seen in tangible forms in the early modern period. As Greenblatt
notes, following the Reformation, Catholic robes and objects were
bought and sold, and were used by actors as costumes in theatrical
performance. What happens when a sacred object such as a bishop's
robe gets used in this way? The investment that theatre companies
made in such objects shows that, beyond the material value of the cloth
itself as a costume, there is also a symbolic value that is retained even
as the robe moves from the church to the stage. But this symbolic
value is also called into question by its new use, held up to the scrutiny
of the audience so that it is possible to ask what the real difference is
between a man who wears a robe in a church and a man who wears
the same robe in a play. This is a version of the 'appropriation' of
cultural objects by the theatre that Greenblatt outlines in his account

of the circulation of social energy. Harsnett's attempt to align exorcism with the theatre is thus an attempt to empty it of its power and significance.

Turning to *King Lear*, Greenblatt proposes that Shakespeare's use of Harsnett's text is unusual precisely because he draws out this link between the debunking of exorcism and the power of theatre. As he notes, it is usual for early modern dramatists to seek the *authentic* in non-fictional texts, for example, in the handbooks of military or legal practices. The playwright wishes to lend an air of realism to his play by drawing on the language of the real world, so that his soldiers sound like soldiers and his lawyers like lawyers. But when Shakespeare uses Harsnett it is to appropriate something that is presented in the source text as fraudulent and *inauthentic*. So in *King Lear* the invocation of the names Obidicut, Hobbididence, Mahu, Modo and Flibbertigibbet (4.1), and the disguise of Edgar as the madman Poor Tom, gain power because they are unbelievable. The devils sound ridiculous, and the behaviour of the one possessed by devils is similarly unconvincing. The strategies adopted by Edgar in the play are supposed to work upon other characters within the play, but the audience is never in any doubt that these strategies are simply an illusion: 'we enjoy being brazenly lied to, we welcome for the sake of pleasure what we know to be untrue, but we withhold from the theater the simple assent we grant to everyday reality' (1990: 119). The theatre invites us to be complicit with its illusions, not to believe in them. As in Harsnett's criticism of the exorcists, in *King Lear* rituals and beliefs are shown to be empty; whenever characters call upon the gods for help they receive no answer, and the suffering that they undergo is given a decidedly human rather than divine source.

To this point, Greenblatt wants to argue for the similarity in effect of Harsnett's text and Shakespeare's play. Both see exorcism, possession and demons as illusory, and both see the rituals that are supposed to respond to these phenomena as theatrical performances. But as in some of his earlier comments, Greenblatt turns the argument again, suggesting that the transposition of the 'same' material from one realm to another – as in the movement of a religious robe from the church to the stage – enacts a transformation of that material. Represented on the stage, Harsnett's arguments are 'alienated' from themselves (1990: 120). Part of the problem comes from the fact that illusion tends to be used by sympathetic characters such as Edgar. But part of it comes from the sense that even if we accept that there are no demons and that human suffering is the result of human action, this is hardly reassuring. *King Lear* is, after all, one of Shakespeare's greatest tragedies, and the destruction and pain that Lear, Gloucester and others endure is not lessened by the fact that it does not spring from a supernatural source. That Lear's suffering stems from Lear's own mistakes in dividing his family and kingdom at the beginning of the play doesn't diminish that suffering. It might not be possible to make devils appear on the stage, but no benevolent supernatural force appears either. Just as the ritual of exorcism testifies to a desire to redeem those apparently possessed by devils, so Shakespeare's play creates a craving for the redemption of the suffering of Lear, most evident in the desperate scenes in which he seeks to revive Cordelia and the audience too wishes to see her resurrected. That this redemption is not forthcoming amounts to an emptying out of the official religious position, represented by Harsnett, that wishes to preserve the true Christian redemption by separating it from the false, illusory redemptions of exorcism. The theatre attempts to restage what Harsnett has apparently demystified. As Greenblatt comments: 'evacuated rituals, drained of their original meaning, are preferable to no rituals at all' (1990: 127). Again, there is an echo of *Renaissance Self-Fashioning* in which he concludes that although we recognize that human autonomy is a fiction, nonetheless it remains a fiction in which we would like to be able to believe.

Ultimately, Greenblatt proposes, Shakespeare is writing in the service of only one institution: the theatre. And in staging the apparently fraudulent rituals of exorcism, he is doing so within an institution that is based upon fraudulent representation. The theatre empties out everything that appears on its stage precisely because it doesn't ask anyone to believe that those appearances are reality. As such, it asks its audiences to believe in nothing other than theatre. It is this, for Greenblatt, that allows theatre to survive the institutions that it represents, always negotiating new relationships with new institutions, but in turn emptying out those institutions. This does not entail an escape from an embeddedness in the specific relations within a culture, but is instead a process of creation and re-creation within changing contexts.

The intensity or energy that Greenblatt seeks to explain, the ability, that is, for Shakespeare's plays to appeal to audiences who share little of the culture in which and for which he wrote, seems to reside in

ALIENATION

The concept of alienation has been widely used, particularly by Marxist critics. Deriving from Marx's writings, whose own thinking on alienation is based in the German philosopher G. W. F. Hegel's (1770–1831) notion of the 'unhappy consciousness' (see Hegel 1967), most versions of alienation involve ideas of a sense of the self being divided or estranged from some aspect of the world. For Hegel, it is necessary for consciousness to be unified, in the sense that the way one acts in the world is consistent with one's own sense of one's essence or identity. This is only possible within a social space which is itself rational and without contradictions, and thus there is an agreement between how one appears within a community (appearance), how one thinks of oneself (essence), and what one does (action). Consciousness becomes unhappy when such agreement is not possible, particularly when the demands of society force an individual into actions that contradict his or her own sense of self-identity. When Greenblatt uses the word alienation in this context, he also draws here on the legal sense of alienation as a loss of ownership.

Greenblatt links his discussion of *King Lear* to the 'alienation-effect' (or *Verfremdungseffekt*) of the German playwright, poet and director Bertolt Brecht (1898–1956) (Greenblatt 1990: 126). Brecht proposed that theatre should not invite the audience members to suspend their disbelief or to empathize with the characters on stage. Equally, an actor should not identify with the role that he or she plays. The purpose of this is to encourage the audience to take a critical and detached stance towards what they see, and to learn something from a performance rather than merely sympathize with the plight of a character. So the audience will be drawn into the performance, but should never forget that what they are watching is a theatrical performance, and that those on stage are actors. Actors thus address the audience 'out of character' as well as speaking the lines of the play. Brecht's plays thus highlight their own status as theatre, drawing attention to their own artificiality, and, by extension, to the artificiality of the conventions of theatre itself.

this 'desire for spectacular impostures' (1990: 128). In other words, we like being lied to, we like fraudulent illusions, because they carry with them the promise of something that we would like to believe in. Even if we know that we can never attain the redemption that theatre holds out to us, even if it tells us that those who claim to offer us redemption are frauds and theatrical tricksters, the desire for that redemption is real enough. Theatre, through its self-conscious fraudulence, nonetheless reveals the truth of this desire.

SUMMARY

In Greenblatt's second major book, *Shakespearean Negotiations*, he raises the question of the intensity of works of literature, and especially Shakespeare's theatre. Asking where this power over the audience comes from, Greenblatt outlines a conception of 'social energy', charting the varied negotiations between the stage and the non-theatrical world. Greenblatt's reading of Shakespeare's *Henry IV* plays and *Henry V* open up his argument on subversion and containment, in which subversive energies are provoked so that they may be contained by an authority or institution. Relating Shakespeare's plays to colonial texts, Greenblatt argues that religion is used as part of the colonial enterprise. In his reading of *King Lear*, he extends this through an analysis of the relation between belief and disbelief around the ritual of exorcism, arguing that although theatre reveals itself as a fraudulent illusion, it also shows that other institutions which hold out the promise of redemption are similarly illusory.

5

RESONANCE AND
WONDER

AN UNANTICIPATED AESTHETIC DIMENSION

When Gallagher and Greenblatt come to characterize their approach
to extending the boundaries of art in the name of a broad concept of
culture, they admit that this undermines many of the central pre-
suppositions of aesthetics, in particular those which stress the originality
and genius of the artist. This does not amount to giving up on the idea
of aesthetic response, however. On the contrary, 'wonder' appears in
their response to objects that would not normally be of interest to the
cultural critic:

> In the analysis of the larger cultural field, canonical works of art are brought
> into relation not only with works judged as minor, but also with texts that are
> not by anyone's standards literary. The conjunction can produce almost
> surrealist wonder at the revelation of an unanticipated aesthetic dimension in
> objects without pretensions to the aesthetic.
>
> (Gallagher and Greenblatt 2000: 10)

The consequence of this is that the literary text 'loses exclusive rights
to the experience of wonder' (2000: 12). Wonder, then, is not evap-
orated by new historicism, it is 'democratized', in that it is to be found
in a wide variety of objects that cannot be attributed to the work of
a specific, special individual. What exactly is this 'wonder'?

In Chapter 2, I proposed that one of the central issues to arise from Stephen Greenblatt's work was precisely the question of the aesthetic. In that earlier chapter, I suggested that one of the key ways into thinking about how the aesthetic functions in new historicism was to be found through the references in *Practicing New Historicism* to romantic thinkers such as the philosopher Johann Gottfried von Herder (1744–1803). Later in this chapter, I will return to these invocations of Herder's work in order to show what exactly it is that Greenblatt takes from him. This will allow us to deepen our sense of the aesthetic thought within new historicism, providing the context for a discussion of the connected ideas of resonance and wonder.

The two terms 'resonance' and 'wonder' are central both to an essay that bears this title, included in *Learning to Curse*, and to Greenblatt's book *Marvelous Possessions: The Wonder of the New World* (1991). At the end of 'Resonance and Wonder', Greenblatt quotes a passage from the medieval thinker Albert the Great (also known as Albertus Magnus, 1193?–1280) in which he gives a powerful definition of wonder (which Greenblatt also alludes to in 2001: 107–8 and at several points in *Marvelous Possessions*):

> wonder is defined as a constriction and suspension of the heart caused by amazement at the sensible appearance of something so portentous, great, and unusual, that the heart suffers a systole [a contraction]. Hence wonder is something like fear in its effect on the heart. This effect of wonder, then, this constriction and systole of the heart, spring from an unfulfilled but felt desire to know the cause of that which appears portentous and unusual: so it was in the beginning when men, up to that time unskilled, began to philosophize. . . . Now the man who is puzzled and wonders apparently does not know. Hence wonder is the movement of the man who does not know his way of finding out, to get at the bottom of that at which he wonders and to determine its cause. . . . Such is the origin of philosophy.
>
> (Quoted in Greenblatt 1992: 181)

Greenblatt proposes that this sense of amazement and desire also lies at the heart of his own critical endeavours. Socrates, often regarded as the founding figure of Western philosophy, proposed that philosophy begins in wonder (cited in Greenblatt 1991: 19). But whereas philosophy might strive to replace this sense of amazement with a secure knowledge of its cause – to move then from the unknown to the known – 'it is the function of the new historicism continually to renew the marvelous at the heart of the resonant' (1992: 181). Rather than explaining, and explaining away, the effect of wonder, new historicism seeks to repeat and intensify this effect for the reader.

What should also be noted, however, is the doubled sense of wonder in the definition here. Wonder is first of all a physical effect on the body, a disturbance to the rhythm of the heart, a feeling something like fear. This becomes a mental process; the one who is physically affected begins to wonder about it. But it is clear that the experience of wonder in this account precedes knowledge of what has caused it. There is thus something involuntary about wonder, it is a response that does not come from an intellectual process, but instead is that which sets intellectualization in motion. In this respect, wonder resembles other emotional responses such as pleasure, laughter, uneasiness, delight, discomfort and even boredom. The ways in which these responses might be triggered are many and various, and they are often accompanied by surprise. In thinking about this as an aesthetic response, it is necessary to remember that *aisthesis* (the Greek root of 'aesthetic') is primarily concerned with sensation, and with the impact of the world upon the senses. So aesthetics retains a sense of relation to the world and its objects, and of response to that relation, in particular what they make us feel. Attempts to understand such responses, and to understand the objects that cause them, must always be to some extent belated or deferred, in that understanding must be derived from reflection on an experience that has already occurred. What this implies is a gap in our knowledge, a sense that we have encountered something that could not have been predicted. As Greenblatt puts it in *Marvelous Possessions*: 'the experience of wonder continually reminds us that our grasp of the world is incomplete' (1991: 24).

Wonder is, of course, one of the effects of art, of literature and of theatrical presentation. The elements of pleasure and of emotional response that are aroused by literature, in particular, are clearly conveyed throughout Greenblatt's work, but as might be expected from a critic whose notion of culture has always extended beyond the conventional categories of art, other forms of cultural production are also seen to be capable of producing such effects. In 'Resonance and Wonder', much of the discussion centres on the role of objects in museums. There is a conventional form of museum display, remarks Greenblatt, that seems to be designed to encourage wonder; the great work of art is presented for lengthy viewing and contemplation, offered up as an object of veneration and desire. But this is precisely in order to assert that such an object cannot be possessed, he argues; unique and most often literally untouchable, the work of art testifies only to its own qualities and to the superlative nature of the one who created it: 'What the work possesses is the power to arouse wonder, and that power, in the dominant aesthetic ideology of the West, has been infused into it by the creative genius of the artist' (1992: 178). This power seems to be possessed by the work itself, so that the art-object appears to escape possession even by the museum that displays it.

For Greenblatt, there is something about this veneration, this worship of the art-object as an isolated and self-contained thing of wonder that runs counter to his sense of culture. While he does see his attitude to works of art as being characterized by wonder, he wishes to extend that sense to objects that normally lie beyond the boundaries of art. In this sense, the aesthetic dimension is 'unanticipated' because spectators expect art to produce such effects, but not necessarily that which is characterized as non-art. If art is a specific form of cultural production, and if it occupies a particular place within a culture, it nonetheless stands in relation to other forms of production, and to the places and spaces allotted to those forms. Without abandoning the benefits that may accrue even within the conventional sense of wonder, Greenblatt needs to introduce a second term to take account of his extended sense of aesthetic response: resonance.

RESONANCE

Resonance was a term that appeared in Greenblatt's works at several points before its full elaboration (see, for example, the long quotation from the opening of *Shakespearean Negotiations* that I looked at in Chapter 4, in which Greenblatt sees resonance as related to the trace of a 'lost life'). In 'Resonance and Wonder', Greenblatt again uses a museum in order to clarify his thinking on the relation between his two central terms. Where wonder was associated with the display of an object such that it seemed to be in isolation from the world that surrounded and produced it, resonance is much more firmly a matter of relation to that world:

> By resonance I mean the power of the object displayed to reach out beyond its formal boundaries to a larger world, to evoke in the viewer the complex,

dynamic cultural forces from which it has emerged and for which as metaphor
or more simply as metonymy it may be taken by a viewer to stand.

(1992: 170)

It is resonance with which the new historicism has an obvious affinity,
in that it always seeks to locate the traces of the world that an object
bears.

In order to demonstrate the differences between a museum based
on wonder and one based on resonance, Greenblatt describes the State
Jewish Museum in Prague. Such exhibitions display not only the great
works of art to be found in conventional art museums, but also offer
up more everyday objects, including those that have been damaged and
defaced. These objects bear the marks of their use, of their involvement
with historical processes as momentous as wars and as pedestrian as
accidental breakages, as well as the marks of attempts to reform them
for another use or context. As Greenblatt puts it: 'wounded artifacts
may be compelling not only as witnesses to the violence of history but
as signs of use, marks of the human touch, and hence links with the
openness to touch that was the condition of their creation' (1992:
172). The wounds that an object displays necessarily conjure up
explanations, narratives that seek to account for them, and thus lead
the viewer to take account of the relationships that have governed the
movement of the object. But in talking about the physical aspects of
the creation of objects, Greenblatt is also recalling the idea of poetics
as a form of making (see p. 29 above), and opening up such objects
to description and interpretation through cultural poetics.

What the State Jewish Museum in Prague conjures up is not so
much veneration of the objects themselves, but instead a memory of
those who possessed and used them. That the Museum occupies several
synagogues in Prague that are no longer used for religious purposes
intensifies the sense of the loss of a people, as much as it connotes the
survival of artefacts. Many of the objects that the museum contains are
not in themselves remarkable, but they attain their resonance through
their connection to the now silent voices of those who were caught
up in the repeated violence against the Jews in Prague, most obviously
during the period of Nazi control of Czechoslovakia in the 1940s.
Greenblatt notes the irony of the fact that many of these artefacts
survived only because they were confiscated and stored by the Nazis.
Indeed, the Museum's collections were the result of a desire on the

part of the Nazi authorities to understand Jewish culture, or what was called the 'Jewish Question', and to mount exhibitions of Jewish artefacts acquired largely from those who had been sent to concentration camps. The 'memorial complex' that the museum now forms is thus impure in several senses; it testifies to the violence and desecration to which Jewish culture was exposed; it marks the absence of those to whom the objects belonged; and it pays homage to their memories.

For Greenblatt, however, resonance is not necessarily bound up with violence and absence. It is evoked, he suggests, by any objects that imply 'a larger community of voices and skills, an imagined ethnographic thickness' (1992: 176). This phrase is telling, partly because of its invocation of the thick description of Geertz discussed in Chapter 2, and partly because it calls this ethnographic thickness 'imagined'. Imagination becomes increasingly emphasized in Greenblatt's work, as I will show in Chapter 6, and so I won't say much about it here. But it presents a problem for Greenblatt in that, as he admits at the end of this essay, the choice between resonance and wonder is too stark. In fact, he proposes that the most successful exhibitions are probably those that arouse wonder, and this may be partly because the experience of wonder does not require an effort of the imagination. It simply happens, and in that sense it is an unwilled response. Resonance also has an emotional dimension, but it is mediated by the need to seek an explanation, or to know something of the context of the objects exhibited. This knowledge might exist prior to visiting the museum, but it often comes from the framing devices that museums employ, such as written captions, guidebooks, tours and audio guides. This might remind us of the difference that Walter Benjamin notes in different forms of story-telling (see pp. 36–8 above): some stories are told merely for their intrinsic interest (wonder), others come already framed by an interpretation, like those often found in newspapers (resonance). Nonetheless, surprise, veneration and emotional response allow for a movement from wonder to resonance, precisely because (as Albertus Magnus says) wonder leads to a desire to know what it is that has aroused this effect. An object that creates wonder can lead the viewer to think about the cultural moments to which it is connected, to ask who made it, how it was made, and how it has been used in the years since its production. It is harder to be surprised by something that has already been understood. Consequently, it is easier to move from wonder to resonance than the other way around.

POLITICS, AESTHETICS AND ROMANTICISM

There is an objection to be made to all of this. If an unanticipated aesthetic dimension is potentially to be found in *any* object, then does this mean that an entire culture becomes 'aestheticized'? This argument is most frequently based on an essay by Walter Benjamin on 'The Work of Art in the Age of Its Technological Reproducibility' (see my comments on Benjamin above, p. 37). At the conclusion of this essay, Benjamin famously states that 'The logical outcome of fascism is an aestheticizing of political life' and that 'All efforts to aestheticize politics culminate in one point. That one point is war' (Benjamin 2003: 269). What is meant by 'aestheticization' is that a state is organized in such a way that society itself is regarded as a work of art. That is, it is treated as a thing of beauty, and the prime example of this is when a society goes to war. War is the culmination of an aestheticized politics because it is the point at which there is a profound unity within a society and the state takes on a sacred aspect. War itself is seen to be beautiful, again taking on the characteristics of art, and is seen to be worthy of sacrifice. Wartime propaganda often exploits such notions, even in non-fascist states. One famous response to this kind of thinking in English poetry is Wilfred Owen's (1893–1918) refusal in 'Dulce Et Decorum Est' to accept the idea that it is sweet (dulce) and fitting (decorum) to die for one's country.

Noting the 'theory crime' that new historicism is alleged to have committed in its apparent aestheticization of culture, Gallagher and Greenblatt counter in *Practicing New Historicism* that:

> our effort is not to aestheticize an entire culture, but to locate inventive energies more deeply inter-fused within it. To do so is hardly to endorse as aesthetically gratifying every miserable, oppressive structure and every violent action of the past. Rather, it is to imagine that the writers we love did not spring up from nowhere and that their achievements must draw upon a whole life-world and that this life-world has undoubtedly left other traces of itself.

(2000: 12–13)

So, while they are prepared to attribute aesthetic effects to objects and practices that are not usually associated with art, nonetheless this does not amount to suggesting that every aspect of a culture possesses this aesthetic potential. To recognize an aesthetic dimension within an object does not imply acceptance of, or agreement with, the values and structures of the culture in which the object was produced.

As I suggested in my earlier discussion of Benjamin, his work is a frequent reference point for Greenblatt, and so this argument is not simply rejected. Instead, Gallagher and Greenblatt want to say that what they are doing is not susceptible to this criticism. Just as Greenblatt wants to argue for a notion of resonance that is not only evoked by objects that testify to violence and suffering, so the sense of an aesthetic dimension to non-artistic objects does not entail the celebration of violence in past cultures, nor does it suggest that such objects and documents are themselves artworks. One of the defining features of the difference between artistic and non-artistic works is to be located in the connection between wonder and pleasure. As Greenblatt argues, pleasure is 'part both of my own response (for pleasure and what I have called disturbance are often identical) and of what I most wish to understand' (1992: 9). Pleasure, like wonder, prompts interpretation. This interpretation can often be antagonistic to the values and fantasies presented in the works themselves. So while it is argued that there is no desire to reduce the power of the artwork in new historicism, this does not mean that there is an endorsement of the artwork and the values that it represents implied in discussion of it. Gallagher and Greenblatt talk of the writers they love, but they also speak of the need to 'imagine' (that word again) the life-world from which those writers emerged in order to analyse the relation between the text and that world.

The idea of the life-world takes us back to German romantic thought. In particular, in *Practicing New Historicism*, it takes us to the work of Johann Gottfried von Herder (1744–1803). Herder is fundamentally historicist, in that he treats literature and language as the product of a specific place and time. Thus, he relates the character of a national literature to the character of a language, and that language, in turn, is conditioned by the nature of the nation as a geographical location and as a people:

> If then each original language which is the native growth of a country develops in accordance with its climate and region, if each national language forms itself in accordance with the ethics and manner of thought of its people, then conversely, a country's literature which is original and national must form itself in accordance with such a nation's original native language in such a

> way that the two run together. The literature grew up in the language, and the language in the literature; unfortunate is the hand that wants to tear the two apart, deceptive the eye that wants to see the one without the other.
>
> (Herder 2002: 50)

Herder ties together literature, language, land and people. Climate and culture are aspects of the 'originality' of a nation and its cultural products. What Herder's work offers is a clear sense that culture is specific to a given moment in history. Thus when he comes to address the common connection made in the late eighteenth century between Greek culture and that of other periods, Herder stresses that the moment that produced Socrates, Sophocles or Homer is not one that could be repeated or continued as such. Any comparison between a Greek figure and a later one could work only by analogy, not by identity; they could be similar, but not the same. As he puts it, 'Shakespeare was no Sophocles, Milton no Homer . . . yet they were in their kind and place what those were in theirs' (Herder 1997: 291). So Shakespeare could occupy a certain position or fulfil a certain function in his own time, but this does not mean that his plays were equal to those of Sophocles, who was widely thought of in Herder's time as the greatest of dramatists in human history.

What Greenblatt takes from Herder is, first, this historicist insistence on the differences between artistic forms that derive from their different locations. Thus Sophocles and Shakespeare both write tragedies, but the fact of their existing in different times and nations means that tragedy is not the same thing in both cases, even if it appears to fulfil the same function in their respective cultures. An overarching 'theory' of tragedy, then, will cover over rather than reveal these differences. As Gallagher and Greenblatt express one of the consequences of following Herder: 'The task of understanding then depends not on the extraction of an abstract set of principles, and still less on the application of a theoretical model, but rather on an encounter with the singular, the specific, and the individual' (2000: 6). This insight is part of what lies behind the refusal of new historicists to present a set of theoretical principles, and Herder's work also underpins the idea that all of the written and visual traces within a given culture are comprehensible as elements in a network in which each part bears a relation to all the others (see the discussion in 2000: 5–8 and 13).

In order to see what else Greenblatt takes from romantic thought, however, I want to move away from Herder and return to the notion of wonder. Wonder has a double emphasis, as I have already said. On the one hand, wonder is a property of objects; something is seen to be wonderful. But on the other, wonder is the affect that is produced in someone who encounters the object, that is, wonder is a feeling as much as a fact. Here we can begin to see again the romantic inheritance. One of the most pervasive senses of the influence of romantic thought, drawing especially on Kant and Hegel (most obviously Kant 1987 and Hegel 1998), is the idea that art offers a way of understanding the relation between our perception of objects in the world and our ability to judge and comprehend those objects (for an anecdote on Kant, see Greenblatt 1997). In other words, one of the crucial questions within romanticism was to try to demonstrate the unity of what we feel about objects with what we know about them. Our judgement of art, for instance, implies being able to distinguish between good and bad art, but this in turn implies that we can know artworks as they really are, and that our perception of them is accurate. If romanticism is conceived of in part as an attempt to unify a subject's experience of the world with the objects of the world itself, if subject and object are 'unified' in consciousness, then wonder seems to be an exemplary instance of that possibility. The object is wonderful, and this is something that I can know about it, but at the same time, wonder denotes how I feel about the object. Thus my feeling and my knowledge go together, they are unified, and my feeling contains an element of truth because it reflects the true nature of the object. The aesthetic dimension of art – and in new historicism, non-art – becomes of crucial importance because it holds out the promise of aligning knowledge and perception. In Greenblatt's terms, this is implied in the movement from wonder to resonance.

Nevertheless, despite a certain affinity between aspects of romantic thought and Greenblatt's work, there are also some clear differences. Gallagher and Greenblatt note the disastrous reading of an insistence on the relation between culture, a people and national soil that may be seen in the rise of fascism in Germany (2000: 13). Greenblatt also sees the traditional idea of understanding literature in national (or nationalistic) terms as one that has been weakened within literary studies: 'for a professor of English literature, teaching Shakespeare in the later twentieth century at a state university by the waters of the Pacific [the

University of California, Berkeley], the model of literary nationalism seems increasingly irrelevant' (1997: 462). The irrelevance of a national model to Greenblatt's own work is evident in his readings of Shakespeare and English culture through texts from other parts of Europe (as in the examples of the Algonquins, Martin Guerre, Montaigne, Menocchio, and so on) and especially in his relation of early modern European culture to encounters with the New World.

MARVELOUS POSSESSIONS

When Greenblatt comes to discuss the nature of wonder in *Marvelous Possessions*, the sense of a relationship between the one who interprets and that which is interpreted takes on a particular resonance in the context of colonial encounters between European and non-European peoples. In particular, in this book Greenblatt analyses the narratives of travel and discovery that relate those encounters, but, as we might expect, he does not do so in order to provide an overarching history. In fact, the style of this book continues and deepens his use of the fragmentary histories provided by especially striking moments in these narratives: 'It will not escape anyone who reads this book that my chapters are constructed largely around anecdotes, what the French call *petites histoires*, as distinct from the *grand récit* of totalizing, integrated, progressive history, a history that knows where it is going' (1991: 2). This is attributable to the ways in which early modern travel narratives themselves work, not presenting a narrative that is uniformly interesting and well-shaped, but instead offering glimpses of objects, practices and people that provoke a certain fascination. These narratives achieve their strongest effects 'in the shock of the unfamiliar, the provocation of an intense curiosity, the local excitement of discontinuous wonders'. Greenblatt continues:

> Hence they present the world not in stately and harmonious order but in a succession of brief encounters, random experiences, isolated anecdotes of the unanticipated. For the anecdote, which is linked at least etymologically with the unpublished, is the principal register of the unexpected and hence of the encounter with difference that is at once initiated and epitomized by Columbus's marvelous landfall in an unimagined hemisphere that blocked his access to the eastern end of the known world.

> (1991: 2–3)

This paragraph brings together several elements that we have already seen: wonder, the anecdote, the unanticipated, and the relation of the known to the unknown. Like Columbus, and unlike progressive models of history, as Greenblatt reads these narratives he doesn't know where he is going, and this allows for the unexpected, unanticipated experience of wonder to emerge through the surprise of the anecdote.

What Greenblatt shows in this book is that any encounter between people of different cultural backgrounds is determined to a great degree by the interpretative strategies employed by the participants. This insight leads him to pose a series of questions:

> How does one read the signs of the other? How does one make signs to the other? How does one reconcile the desire for transparent signs with the opacity of an unknown culture? How does one move from mute wonder to communication? . . . The three modes of communication – mute signs, material exchange, and language – are in turn bound up in a larger question: how is it possible for one system of representation to establish contact with a different system?
>
> (1991: 91)

The encounters that Greenblatt describes act as a kind of allegory for the role of the critic. Just as the participants in an encounter between two cultures must seek a way of 'translating' the sign systems of the other, and of translating their own modes of communication so that they might be understood by the other, so the critic is similarly confronted by the need to read the signs of the other, and to communicate that reading. One of the solutions to this problem of making contact, and of finding a space in which it is possible for some kind of exchange to occur, is improvisation. As in *Renaissance Self-Fashioning*, improvisation is a way for an individual to come to some accommodation with the situation in which he or she operates. Improvisation, here defined as 'the ability to insert the self in the sign systems of others' (1991: 98), frequently takes the form of a kind of imitation or mimesis. This imitation of the behaviour, rituals and practices of another culture allows an exchange to take place even where there is no shared language and there are no common cultural understandings. Beyond the evident differences between the people of two different cultures (whether that difference appears in physical appearance, customs, dress, possessions, language, religious beliefs, political organization and so on), nevertheless a mimetic appropriation of those differences remains possible, that is, they can be copied or mimicked, so that sufficient likeness can be asserted for some sort of relation to be possible. In this way, the Europeans who travelled to the new world were able to trade with the indigenous peoples that they encountered almost from the moment of their arrival, despite a virtually total and reciprocal incomprehension.

MIMESIS

The concept of mimesis has been extremely influential in a range of disciplines, and has frequently been used to explain the relationship of representations to that which is represented. Despite, or perhaps because of, its widespread use, the concept of mimesis remains vague, and can encompass everything from aesthetic practices to aspects of everyday behaviour. Traditional conceptions of mimesis stress similarity, in that the representation is thought of as an image or imitation of an original. In Plato's *Republic*, Socrates famously criticizes poets because their work is always ultimately imitative, and is thus at a 'remove' from truth, copying objects in the world that are themselves only an image of the ideal form of an object. Socrates' view has been consistently challenged, but the idea that art is ultimately a kind of copying of the world, and thus less 'real', has persisted. A more positive account is given by Aristotle, who makes mimesis central to his *Poetics*. Certainly the idea of imitating models, especially those offered by ancient Greek and Roman culture, was central to artistic thinking and practice in the early modern period. Greene suggests that 'The imitation of models was a precept and an activity which during that era embraced not only literature but pedagogy, grammar, rhetoric, esthetics, the visual arts, music, historiography, politics, and philosophy' (1982: 1). What has emerged in more recent work on mimesis is an attention to the differences between the object and the representation. As Melberg puts it: '*Mimesis* is inherently and always already a *repetition* – meaning that *mimesis* is always the meeting-place of two opposing but connected ways of thinking, acting and making: similarity and difference' (1995: 1). While the literature on mimesis is enormous, see Auerbach 1968; Cohen 1994; Gebauer and Wulf 1995; Girard 1988 and Melberg 1995.

Greenblatt places his notion of mimesis in a specific context, relating it to capitalism: 'the problem of the assimilation of the other is linked to what we may call, adapting Marx, *the reproduction and circulation of mimetic capital*' (1991: 6). There are three reasons, Greenblatt proposes, to link mimesis and capital. What he focuses on is mimesis as the production of images, and capitalism as the social and economic structure within which those images circulate. Mimesis is thus related to capitalism due to the proliferation, reproduction and circulation of images in a global context. Greenblatt conveys a sense of a stockpile of representations, a set of symbols and symbolic relations awaiting use in producing new representations, that is, open to the forms of appropriation discussed in *Shakespearean Negotiations*. Further, he argues that mimesis is itself 'a social relation of production':

I take this to mean that any given representation is not only the reflection or product of social relations but that it is itself a social relation, linked to the group understandings, status hierarchies, resistances, and conflicts that exist in other spheres of the culture in which it circulates. This means that representations are not only products but producers, capable of decisively altering the very forces that brought them into being.

(1991: 6)

Representation, then, does not merely 'reflect' reality. Reality is produced by and as representation, feeding back into the system from which the representation emerged, and altering that system as it does so. This does not mean that everything may be collapsed into this sense of mimetic reproduction, however. Representation and reality are not the same thing, but one cannot be isolated from the other.

One example of this process of feeding back is the changed sense of the Europeans' own projects that may be discerned in the narratives of New World encounters. Greenblatt is keen that his readers understand that in reading these narratives the critic will not be given a 'true' picture of the New World itself. Even positive descriptions of the places and peoples that the travellers found should be read primarily for what they tell us about the values and beliefs that inform the construction of those descriptions, representations and narratives: 'We can be certain only that European representations of the New World tell us something about the European practice of representation' (1991: 7). Writing itself is seen to be one of the European 'technologies', to be part of the European power that manifested itself in the New World encounters:

> The Europeans who ventured to the New World in the first decades after
> Columbus's discovery shared a complex, well-developed, and, above all, mobile
> technology of power: writing, navigational instruments, ships, war-horses, attack
> dogs, effective armor, and highly lethal weapons, including gunpowder.
>
> (1991: 9)

This is a telling sentence, and a disarming one. In reading the items
in this list it is easy to pass over the logic that connects them. What
exactly is the link between writing and attack dogs?

The answer to this question lies in the notion of technology. As in
the discussion of technology in Chapter 1 (see pp. 18–21), it is necessary
to think of it in two ways; first, in our more usual modern sense of
instruments that allow us to gain some control over the world and its
events (navigational instruments, armour, ships, weapons, and so on),
but also in the wider sense of *technē*, that is, of an 'art' in a broad sense.
The art of war is related to the art of writing in its capacity for revealing
a difference between the 'advanced' Europeans and the 'savage' or
'barbarous' inhabitants of the New World. Just as weapons allow for
a physical dominance that shows a supposed superiority over weaker
opponents, so the possession of writing is also seen to be a mark of
superiority. Such a perception, of course, rests on the belief that those
cultures encountered do not possess writing, or some equivalent form
of symbolic representation. As Greenblatt suggests, there is also an
economic dimension to all of this, and it takes us back to the idea of
mimesis. The printing press is described by Greenblatt as 'the age's
greatest technological device for the circulation of mimetic capital'
(1991: 8). As in *Shakespearean Negotiations*, circulation becomes a key
term, since it allows Greenblatt to link different areas and practices of
a culture. But it also shows the necessary relation between a 'discovered'
culture and that which does the discovering. As Greenblatt argues:

> Mimetic circulation . . . is double: first, representations and the particular
> technologies that generate them are carried from place to place, most often
> moving according to the logic of conquest and trade though occasionally
> swerving in unforeseen directions, propelled by perversity or accident; second,
> those who receive representations from elsewhere themselves move, with
> greater or lesser freedom, among a range of images and techniques simul-
> taneously available in their culture.
>
> (1991: 120)

Technologies of representation are part of the strategies of power that the Europeans use to exert some control over those they encounter in the New World. But these encounters also generate representations that travel back to Europe, and that have an impact upon that culture. Like art or literature, then, these representations are not merely reflections of the world; they become bound up in the structures that shape the world, they become part of people's lives. Culture is mobile, shifting and contested. While there is circulation, such circulation is never absolutely free, and there are always structures of value and of cultural identity that determine both the boundaries and how they are crossed.

Greenblatt's interest, then, rather than being in how the New World and its inhabitants are represented – and in whether this representation is 'accurate' or not – instead focuses on European responses to the encounter between Europe and the New World. To judge these responses in terms of their accuracy, or even their logicality, would be to misunderstand the nature of the responses and of those who made them: 'Their overriding interest is not knowledge of the other but practice upon the other; and, as I shall try to show, the principal faculty involved in generating these representations is not reason but imagination' (1991: 12–13). *Marvelous Possessions* is one attempt to show the stakes of these acts of imagination, but to understand these ideas fully it is necessary to think in more depth about the role of imagination in Greenblatt's work.

SUMMARY

Resonance and wonder have become key terms in Greenblatt's work, and are fully elaborated in the essay 'Resonance and Wonder' and in *Marvelous Possessions*. Each term reveals a different attitude to objects, wonder encapsulating a sense of surprise that is produced by the encounter with an object, artistic or otherwise. Resonance lacks the immediacy of wonder, demanding an explanation of its context and of the life to which it is, or was, connected. There is a trace in this thinking of an inheritance from German romanticism, especially the work of Herder. Central to this inheritance is an emphasis on a historicized sense of culture, relating it to language and national identity, but there is also a more Kantian move here, in which wonder can be seen to be both the property of an object and the experience of the subject who perceives it. In his work on New World encounters, Greenblatt connects this work on wonder and the aesthetic to practices of representation and to what he calls the circulation of mimetic capital. What is stressed is the way in which an encounter between European and non-European culture works in both directions, reflecting back on Europe as well as impacting on those who are 'discovered'.

6

IMAGINATION
AND WILL

Central to Greenblatt's recent work is the idea of imagination. The term has become increasingly important in the later books, yet it remains something that is best thought of outside of the narrow constraints to which it is often consigned. Imagination, like so many of the other terms that Greenblatt uses (such as culture, the aesthetic, and so on), functions within social modes of interaction that cannot be identified simply with art. As Gallagher and Greenblatt comment in *Practicing New Historicism*: 'The house of the imagination has many mansions, of which art (a relatively late invention as a distinct category) is only one' (2000: 12).

In this chapter, I will be examining the treatment of imagination with respect to two of Greenblatt's books, *Hamlet in Purgatory* (2001) and *Will in the World* (2004). In both, Greenblatt offers engagements with the work and life of Shakespeare, attempting – in ways that will have become familiar from the discussions in earlier chapters of this book – to demonstrate both those cultural influences that helped to shape Shakespeare's work and the shaping of those influences that Shakespeare performed in producing his texts. As in his earlier writings, Greenblatt relates the early modern practices that he is describing and analysing to his own position as a critic, and in both cases imagination becomes a privileged term. As he puts it in *Will in the World*:

> To understand who Shakespeare was, it is important to follow the verbal traces
> he left behind back into the life he lived and into the world to which he was
> so open. And to understand how Shakespeare used his imagination to transform
> his life into his art, it is important to use our own imagination.
>
> (Greenblatt 2004: 14)

Characteristically, there is a double movement here: Greenblatt first wants us to follow verbal traces, the traces that we call Shakespeare's works, into his life and world. The art illuminates the world and the place of the writer within it. As in *Renaissance Self-Fashioning*, at the heart of this project is the life of an individual or subject. This should hardly be a surprise, of course, in a biography. Second, Greenblatt reverses the trajectory, moving from the life to the art. In this dual movement, Greenblatt stresses a similarly dual working of imagination: Shakespeare's own and that of the critic. But what exactly is imagination, and what role does it play in these texts?

IMAGINATION

Imagination has a long critical heritage, and has been valued differently – and defined differently – at different points in history and in different cultures. It is commonly related to ideas of fiction, fantasy, dreams and unreality. That is, it pertains to the mental processes by which it is possible to conjure up things that do not strictly speaking exist in the material way that objects in the world might be said to exist. Imagination is frequently something highly prized as a creative tool, it is the faculty that allows artists and others to envisage things, people, places and ideas that go beyond the 'ordinary' world of everyday experience. It is precisely how 'imaginative' an artist appears to be that is often the object of praise of an artist's work. This does not mean, of course, that the objects of imagination bear no relation to everyday experience, and this is something that comes across clearly in a text such as Thomas More's *Utopia* (as you will remember from Chapter 3). Utopia is a land that may not exist, and the practices of its inhabitants are strikingly different from those of the society that More inhabits. But it is this very distance between the world More occupies and the one that he imagines that provokes the reader into reflecting on her or his own world, and to imagine how that world might itself be different. The imagination of the author sets in motion the imagination of the reader.

Of course, many of the categories that we use in everyday life are themselves the product of imagination. Thus Benedict Anderson can argue in *Imagined Communities*, a book on the concept of nationalism and its historical development, that 'the members of even the smallest nation will never know most of their fellow members, meet them, or even hear of them, yet in the minds of each lives the image of their communion' (1991: 6). This also points towards a more negative conception of imagination, however, and it is often the root of a certain unease. It is frequently associated with lying, falsehood, self-deception (as in the idea of something said to be merely 'imaginary') or with an 'escape' from the real world into the realms of fantasy. As such, imagination has become linked to concepts such as ideology. Ideology becomes tied up with imagination to the extent that it involves a relation to the world that is in large part a mental projection, rather than an 'accurate' perception of the world 'as it really is'. Part of the problem for such notions of ideology is to know securely that the one who claims to see through it is truly in a position that lies outside of ideology and is not simply projecting a different – but equally ideological – point of view.

IMAGINATION'S HISTORY

Central to Western notions of imagination is Aristotle's conception of it as a bridge between sensation and reason. This is so for Aristotle because he sees the mental images that we use in thinking – to understand this try to think of a triangle without picturing one, for example – as related to the objects in the world. All thinking is therefore related to representation, as the mind represents to itself the objects that it is trying to comprehend. This implies that images are a reliable source of information about the objects represented, linking sensory perception and mental processes of understanding. This is the view given in several of Aristotle's texts, most notably *De anima* ('Of the soul') and *De memoria* ('Of memory'). As such, as Richard Kearney puts it, imagination remains largely a reproductive rather than a productive faculty, and it is not the source of what we now think of as 'originality' (Kearney 1988: 113).

Like Aristotle, Greenblatt clearly sees a relation between images of the world and the world 'itself', but his sense of imagination might also again be fruitfully linked to the work of Montaigne. In Montaigne's essay 'On the power of the imagination', he suggests that imagination

IDEOLOGY

Ideology was for some time quite an unfashionable term, partly due to its association with an unsubtle form of Marxism. In its simplest form, ideology is seen as a distortion of the real world. We cannot see the world 'as it really is' because some power operates on us to make us see the world in a particular, and erroneous, way. This view suggests that ideology is a problem not with the way the world actually is but, instead, with how we see it, and this notion of vision is embedded in the origins of the word (it shares its roots with 'idea'). This implies that a change in perception would allow us to get a better sense of the world.

This view of ideology was developed and challenged by the French Marxist philosopher Louis Althusser (1918–90). Althusser argued that ideology was not false perception but perception itself, and was a fundamental part of the experience of being human. Althusser differentiates what he calls a Repressive State Apparatus from an Ideological State Apparatus (ISA). The former works through force, including the actions of the police and armed forces, whereas the latter works through ideology and is invested in private as well as public institutions, such as the family. Ideology works to produce the kind of people needed by a particular social organization, most obviously capitalism, by making individuals recognize their place within a social structure through a kind of hailing or calling that he calls interpellation. There are clearly some parallels between what Althusser calls ideology and what Greenblatt calls culture, since Greenblatt's notion of culture also includes restraints that are enforced both in formal ways by institutions and in informal ways by the approval and disapproval of others.

The idea of ideological critique has been contested from many quarters. One of the most pressing problems for anyone who claims to have 'seen through' ideology is in proving that their own view of the world is not simply another ideological position, that their view is genuinely a demystification rather a remystification. For some of the most challenging work on ideology in recent years, see Žižek 1989 and 1994.

– including his own – is such a powerful force that it can produce physical effects, and this can result in illness or even death:

Some there are who forestall the hand of their executioners; one man was on the scaffold, being un-blindfolded so that his pardon could be read to him, when he fell down dead, the blow being struck by his imagination alone. When imaginary thoughts trouble us we break into sweats, start trembling, grow pale or flush crimson; we lie struck supine on our feather-beds and feel our bodies agitated by such emotions; some even die from them.

(1991: 110)

For Montaigne, then, imagination is not confined to mental conceptions of possibilities and is not tied to the world as it really is; such thoughts take on a physical aspect, they make something happen to the one who thinks them. Imagination thus has a similar structure to Greenblatt's ideas of wonder or resonance: in part it prompts thought, but it also contains elements of physical response such as surprise, laughter, fear or anxiety. There is an aesthetic dimension to our fantasies, linking that idea of aesthetic not just to art but to perception. The images produced by imagination don't just represent the world, they impact upon it.

Imagination takes on a crucial dimension in the work of the German philosopher Immanuel Kant (who was discussed in Chapter 5). Kant's thinking on imagination changed over the course of his writings, but there are powerful formulations in his *Critique of Pure Reason*. In trying to account for the ways in which it is possible for a human subject to 'know' the objects of the world, Kant proposes what is known as an idealist position, in contrast to Aristotle's more realist conception of imagination as representation. That is, Kant emphasizes the extent to which knowledge of objects is always a matter of perception, and thus is dependent on the mental faculties and concepts through which people perceive the world. Kant wants to try to develop a more productive sense of imagination than that of Aristotle, and thus he proposes that while our knowledge relies upon sensory experience – knowledge is knowledge of something, and that something is the 'content' of our thinking – the form in which we grasp that knowledge is supplied by the faculty of understanding itself. Without under-standing, our experience of objects merely produces sensation, but understanding must always be an understanding of something, it requires some form of content, and without that content understanding is empty. Crucial to thinking about this relation between sensory experience and understanding is the role that Kant gives to imagination. For Kant, imagination precedes both sensation and understanding, because he argues that it is necessary for us to be aware not only of our perception of an object but also of our own consciousness. In other words, if we are conscious of an object, there must also be a consciousness capable of having that sensation. Imagination is what allows for a 'synthesis' of what appears to the senses with the faculty of understanding, and thus it is imagination that allows sensory experience to become knowledge. Imagination is thus productive and not just reproductive since, as Howard Caygill suggests, the *original* representations that Kant's imagination produces 'are not derived from experience but provide conditions of experience' (Caygill 1995: 248).

This combination of ideas – Aristotle's sense of the imagination as a link between sensation and reason, Montaigne's insistence on the power of the imagination to make things happen in the world, and Kant's notion of a productive imagination that goes beyond represen-tation and reproduction – all underpin Greenblatt's use of imagination. One of the things that characterizes new historicism is the effort to take the imagination, and things imagined, seriously. Gallagher and Greenblatt note that part of what they took from Marxist historians (and especially E. P. Thompson) was the realization that 'the historian must be able to push beyond understanding a past social reality into imagining the social imaginary' (2000: 57). By taking into account the desires and dreams of those who lived a particular social reality, counter-histories emerge, and those counterhistories tell the historian much about the relation of those people to their realities (on counterhistory, see Chapter 2). Imagination is thus able to produce images of the world, to produce images of another possible and desired world, and to bridge the gap between the two.

SPEAKING WITH THE DEAD

One of the most obvious ways in which Greenblatt can be seen to employ imagination is in the profession of his desire to speak with the dead. As I showed in Chapter 4, this animates his earlier book *Shakespearean Negotiations*, and while Greenblatt concedes immediately that it is not possible to create or re-create any genuine dialogue with the dead, nonetheless he also testifies to his own fascination with the intensity that he sees (and feels) in literary 'simulations' of life. Engaging with the imagination of others – writers, artists, and all those whose historical voices have left traces in the living present – prompts the imagination of the one who hears those voices. This, after all, is one of the most satisfying elements in reading literature, that it provokes the imagination of the reader rather than merely displaying the imagination of the author.

When he begins his book on *Hamlet* and the historical dimensions of Purgatory, Greenblatt returns immediately to this idea of intensity. As he plainly states:

> My only goal was to immerse myself in the tragedy's magical intensity. It seems a bit absurd to bear witness to the intensity of *Hamlet*; but my profession [literary criticism] has become so oddly diffident and even phobic about literary power, so suspicious and tense, that it risks losing sight of – or at least failing to articulate – the whole reason anyone bothers with the enterprise in the first place.

> (2001: 4)

Greenblatt's love of literature is never in doubt, here or elsewhere in his work, but here he is also calling into question discourses that talk about literary texts without conveying that sense of fascination, without telling us why we should care about literature at all.

Nonetheless, some readers have found *Hamlet in Purgatory* a difficult book precisely because it takes a long time to reach the explicit reading of the play, and deals largely with non-literary texts in its early chapters. The book begins with an elaboration of the context of Purgatory in the early sixteenth century, moving through a series of controversies about the religious status of Purgatory in the context of the English Reformation. Those Protestant writers who are most opposed to the idea of Purgatory focus on three central issues. First, there is the fact that Purgatory was used by the Church – intending here the Roman Catholic Church – to generate income by offering to say prayers for those souls that upon death went neither to Heaven nor to Hell, but instead entered an in-between realm in which they had to be cleansed of certain sins before being allowed into Heaven. For Purgatory's opponents, this was another aspect of a perceived corruption within the Church. The second aspect was the lack of evidence in the Biblical texts for the existence of Purgatory at all. It was, it seemed, a late arrival in Christian thinking, and Greenblatt suggests that the idea of Purgatory only develops properly in the later Middle Ages. As such, Purgatory came to be regarded as a work of imagination, a piece of poetry. This sense was compounded by the third element in the Protestant suspicion of Purgatory; that those who insisted on its existence tended to have completely different conceptions of what it was like. It would be tempting, then, to see the exploitation of the concept of Purgatory in early modern England as a function of ideology, since it is an apparently imaginary structure that is used to control behaviour. But what interests Greenblatt is that some early modern writers (including the poet and churchman John Donne) stress the poetic dimension of thinking about Purgatory. As Greenblatt notes: 'What we call ideology . . . Renaissance England called poetry' (2001: 46).

In line with his thinking on artistic production as only one of several demonstrations of the imagination at work, however, Greenblatt doesn't see this stress on poetry as being the preserve of those usually called poets. Recognizing the limitations of Protestant thinking on poetics, he nonetheless notes with approval the fact that the Protestants opposed to Purgatory 'grasped clearly that the imagination was not exclusively the inspired work of a tiny number of renowned poets, though it included that work; it was, they thought, a quality diffused, for good or ill, throughout a very large mass of makers' (2001: 50). Purgatory was a collective creation, and it was one designed to work upon the imaginations of the collective of the faithful. Specifically, it was intended to prompt them to consider what happens – and most importantly what happens to them – after death.

Greenblatt proposes that we take the idea that Purgatory is a work of the imagination seriously. That is, he wants us to give credit to the fact that any notion of a world that lies beyond our own must rest upon a degree of imagination. Like Heaven or Hell, Purgatory is a realm to which believers have no direct access and of which they have no experience. As such, to think about Purgatory at all is to employ imaginative tools. To call Purgatory 'poetic', then, is to acknowledge the extent to which it is 'made' as much as given (remembering the roots of the idea of poetry in the Greek *poiesis* that I mentioned in Chapter 1). Greenblatt draws on a quotation from Shakespeare in order to make his point. Commenting on the 'shaping fantasies' that

THE REFORMATION

What came to be called the Reformation in Europe marked a decisive shift in Christian thinking. Often said to have started with the German theologian Martin Luther (1483–1546), the Reformation was motivated primarily by a desire to return to the foundations of a Christian Church that was seen to have been corrupted by the wealth and power of the institution itself. Opposed to the secular power of the Pope, Protestants (those who protested against the current state of the Church) sought to return to simpler forms of worship, and this included the project to translate the Bible into vernacular languages so that believers could have a more direct relationship with God and their faith, rather than relying on a priest who would interpret for them texts that were written in Latin or Greek. One of the consequences of this was the growth in the idea of literacy, so that more people could read the Bible for themselves. Protestants rejected everything that seemed to stand between them and God, and this included the use of art and decoration within churches, the use of icons such as statues of the Virgin Mary, and the richness of clothing of priests and bishops. These matters became the subject of great controversy, and the violence that resulted should not be underestimated. Many were executed either for advocating the new faith or for defending the old ways. Nonetheless, it would not be appropriate to overstate the transformations that took place; for many, probably the majority, the institution may have changed, but their religious practices were shaped as much by custom, familiarity and familial influence as by any official version of religious doctrine. See Bossy 1985; Duffy 1992; Haigh 1993.

characterize lunatics, lovers and poets, Theseus in *A Midsummer Night's Dream* suggests that:

> The Poet's eye, in a fine frenzy rolling,
> Doth glance from heaven to earth, from earth to heaven,
> And as imagination bodies forth
> The forms of things unknown, the poet's pen
> Turns them to shapes, and gives to airy nothing
> A local habitation and a name.
>
> (5.1.5–17, quoted at 2001: 161)

In the Protestant critique of Purgatory as poetry, says Greenblatt, this is precisely the process at work. Poetic imagination aims at a cosmic relevance, it offers a space in which the relation of Heaven to Earth may be worked out, but what it actually works upon are 'things unknown'. Poetry turns these unknown things into specific shapes; it gives them both a place and name. Just as the thought of a purgatorial space must be an act of imagination – since none of those who write or speak of it have any direct experience on which to base their thoughts and images – so the act of speaking and writing about Purgatory gives it a place and name. As Greenblatt notes, in *A Midsummer Night's Dream* 'there are strong hints that dreams and idle fantasies reveal truths that waking consciousness, naively confident in its own grasp of reality, cannot recognize or acknowledge' (2001: 164). The consequences of this are clear. That Purgatory may all be a fiction, indeed that to some extent it *must* all be a fiction, doesn't make the actions that people undertake in the name of this fiction any the less real. Many of those who accepted the purgatorial doctrine, or who wagered that if there was a chance of its being real then it was worth the effort of behaving as if it were real, were encouraged to believe that the world to which their souls would be consigned after death was, in fact, *more* real than the one in which they lived.

STAGING GHOSTS

Central to this problem of evidence for the existence of Purgatory, and central to the link that Greenblatt wants to make between the purgatorial discourse and Shakespeare's plays, is the question of the ghost. Ghosts are another example of 'wonder', since they are things that are both wondrous in themselves and that provoke wonder in those who encounter them (see the discussion of wonder in Chapter 5). In his famous soliloquy 'To be or not to be', Hamlet may claim that death is a bourn from which no traveller returns, but as Greenblatt points out, even within the play that contains this speech there is the presence of one character – the ghost of Hamlet's dead father – that contradicts this view. Ghosts become a crucial dimension of attempts to prove that Purgatory is more than a mere fable or fiction, and also become a defining feature of Shakespeare's plays, never more vividly than in *Hamlet*. The appearance of the ghost, of any ghost, suggests that there is a space between Heaven and Hell because the arrival of the ghost characteristically involves some unfinished business between the living and the dead. Those souls that go to Heaven have no need to come back to the living, having already attained eternal joy. Those that enter Hell are allowed no respite from their torments. So if a ghost comes back to trouble those left behind, this must imply that there is an intermediary 'middle space', that they have neither been irrevocably consigned to damnation nor yet allowed to enter Heaven. In several of Shakespeare's plays, a ghost – or at least the appearance of someone who is initially thought to be a ghost – marks the point at which something has not yet been resolved. In the case of *Hamlet*, this is marked both by the ghost's revelation of the murder of Old Hamlet by his brother Claudius, spurring Hamlet on to revenge, and by the injunction that Hamlet is given to 'remember' his father.

The problem with ghosts, of course, is that they are inherently unbelievable. At several points in Greenblatt's account of the use of ghosts in Shakespeare's plays, he notes how many of the characters thought to be ghosts are, in fact, nothing of the sort. Significantly, the audience or reader is usually well aware of this fact. But the ghost in *Hamlet* is of a different order. This ghost is uncanny (in the sense that I described in Chapter 2). That is, it is strangely familiar, and those who encounter it often remark that it is 'like' the dead king. But they all know that the dead king is precisely dead. So a gap opens up between what they think they securely know – that the body of the king lies in a grave and is certainly not capable of walking around the battlements at night – and this unknown thing that takes on the familiar shape of the king that they remember. As Greenblatt puts it, the ghost is an 'embodied memory' (2001: 212). Hamlet's attitude similarly swings between belief and disbelief that this is the ghost of his dead father, thinking at more than one point that the apparition is instead the devil sent to tempt him into the murder of Claudius, and that this will bring about his own damnation (1.4.20–25 and 2.2.575–6).

What the audience is asked to do in many of the plays, including *Hamlet*, is to suspend disbelief. In the case of Hamlet's problem with the appearance of the ghost, this problem is intensified since the audience is asked to believe either in a ghost or else in a demonic apparition. While giving credence to the existence of demons might have been less of a problem for the average early modern viewer of the play, for

whom good and evil were strongly marked categories within an established religious structure (assuming for a moment that there was such
a thing as an average member of an audience), it is clear that there
would still have been insurmountable difficulties in forgetting entirely
that this was the theatrical representation – conveyed by an all-too-
embodied actor – of a demonic figure. Despite such problems, the
powerful effect of staging ghosts is one to which Shakespeare returned
at several points in his career, and modern audiences still find these
ghost-infested plays the most powerful among his works. So what exactly
is the relation between the religious disputation that Greenblatt outlines
with respect to Purgatory and the effect of his plays?

Greenblatt offers an answer in that Shakespeare may have been
aligned with a process of secularization, in which the plays offered a
version, but a disenchanted one, of the power of religious ritual. There
is a similarity here with the argument about exorcism and theatre in
Shakespearean Negotiations. But here, Greenblatt immediately suggests
that perhaps the opposite case is true: '*Hamlet* immeasurably intensifies
a sense of the weirdness of the theatre, its proximity to certain
experiences that had been organized and exploited by religious institutions and rituals' (2001: 253). So, instead of religion being revealed as
a form of theatrical experience, theatre takes on an intensity akin to
spirituality. While it would be tempting to read in the attitudes expressed
in this and other plays a means by which to resolve the much-pondered
question of Shakespeare's own religious allegiance (Protestant, Catholic,
both at different points in his life, neither, and so on, and on), Greenblatt
instead wants to suggest that it is precisely the cultural investment in
ideas such as that of Purgatory that makes it attractive to Shakespeare
as a dramatist. He suggests that rather than giving evidence of a lurking
Catholic sympathy, Shakespeare's use of these materials allows us to
see that 'At a deep level there is something magnificently opportunistic,
absorptive, even cannibalistic about Shakespeare's art' (2001: 254).
Shakespeare's imagination is thus splendidly impure, drawing on the
resources available to him, transforming those materials into the stuff
of art, but never beginning with a *tabula rasa* (a blank slate) never
imagining a world that was not intimately related to that in which he
and his audiences lived. As much as Shakespeare might be held up as a
great producer of drama, for Greenblatt it is important to stress the
degree to which he was also an exemplary consumer.

WILL *IN* THE WORLD

As is evident from books such as *Renaissance Self-Fashioning*, *Shakespearean Negotiations* and *Hamlet in Purgatory*, Greenblatt is consistently interested in the relation between a writer and the world that he or she inhabits. This makes it easier, perhaps, to recognize the multi-faceted pun in the title of his biography of Shakespeare, *Will in the World*. The question of Shakespeare's 'will' – his first name, his intentional acts, his legacy and, if we follow the punning of the sonnets on this word, his sexual behaviour (where 'will' is related to the sexual organs, male and female) – runs through a series of chapters that broach themes familiar to those who have read Greenblatt's other books.

In his Preface, Greenblatt picks up where *Hamlet in Purgatory* leaves off. 'As a writer', he says of Shakespeare, 'he rarely started with a blank slate; he characteristically took materials that had already been in circulation and infused them with his supreme creative energies' (2004: 13). A few sentences later he proposes that one of the prime characteristics of Shakespeare's texts is 'the touch of the real', a sense of lived experience. This experience, of course, is one of the first problems to confront any biographer of Shakespeare. There is a great deal of evidence of the life of William Shakespeare, but there are still frustrating gaps, and much of the evidence sheds little light on the things that most matter to those drawn to explore the life as a consequence of interest in the texts. Greenblatt's recourse to imagination, then, is both exemplarily modest (many biographers resort to bold and overly general statement to disguise what is at best speculative conjecture) and something of a sleight of hand. Stressing the importance of imagination is a way of lending validity to an approach to the project of writing Shakespeare's life that could not plausibly be conducted in any other way. It is only fitting, then, that the first chapter begins with the words 'Let us imagine . . .' (2004: 23).

Yet, as I have suggested above, imagination has a broader significance for Greenblatt. What he relies upon, as shown by the quotation from this book with which I opened this chapter, is a doubled or dialectical sense of the relation between the work and life. In order to show how this works, I propose to concentrate only on the chapter in which Greenblatt treats Shakespeare's sonnets (Chapter 8: 'Master-Mistress'). The sonnets are a crucial test-case for Greenblatt's method since they have long been read as revealing some kind of biographical narrative, centred upon the relationship between the poet, the young man to whom many of the sonnets are dedicated, the Dark Lady, and one or more rivals to the poet, one of whom is usually seen to be a poet himself. Shakespeare's extraordinary sequence of poems is read, then, as a blend of technical mastery and deeply felt emotional turmoil.

One of the persistent problems that any reader of the sonnets has faced, however, is in trying to identify who is exactly involved in the sequence's portrayal of the experiences that apparently motivate it. Greenblatt's selection of candidates is not particularly original – this is one of the book's strengths, in that it prevents the need for long elaborations of why his theories about the sonnets are more convincing than all the others – but the way in which he ties together the writing of the sonnets and the impact of reading them is ingenious, and it all hinges on the work of imagination and identification.

Chapter 8 begins by asserting the likelihood of Henry Wriothesley, Earl of Southampton, as the dedicatee of the sequence. In the early 1590s, Southampton was being encouraged by those within his family, despite his own reluctance, to marry. One of the ways in which Southampton was asked to rethink his refusal to marry was through poetry. This helps to explain the opening set of seventeen sonnets in Shakespeare's sequence, which are apparently addressed to a narcissistic young man, too much in love with his own beauty and youth to be drawn into matrimony. Rather than criticizing the youth for this narcissism, however, the tactic of these poems is to say that the real problem lies in his not being narcissistic enough. The solution offered is the reproduction of the young man's image through an imaginary child, since children were widely portrayed in writing of this period as 'copies' of their parents, playing on two senses of reproduction, the biological and the artistic. The motivation presented for at least part of the sonnet sequence is that these poems will have a direct effect on the reader – in this case a specific individual for whom they are written – and that in reading the poems the reader will identify himself with the young man portrayed and will consequently alter his behaviour. The imaginary child feeds this imaginary identification. This is the dream of much Renaissance poetry, and the same idea is to be found in the opening sonnet of Sir Philip Sidney's *Astrophil and Stella*, which was, until Shakespeare's, the most prominent sonnet sequence in English. This offers another image of Shakespeare as the consumer of those cultural products that already exist around him.

Imagination is involved in this process in the attempt to provoke an imaginative identification of the reader with the persona portrayed. But these love poems have also been open to imagination in a second sense. In fact, many of the most famous sonnets within the sequence have been taken out of their location within it to become expressions of heterosexual desire (much as they are used today in Britain on Valentine's Day cards). As Greenblatt notes, this process was already under way in the 1620s, and as he puts it 'this ability to be imaginatively transformed, seems part of the poet's own design, a manifestation of his supreme skill at playing this special game' (2004: 235). The sonnets are constructed for two distinct audiences: the first, a specific set of individuals, who will see themselves in the 'characters'; second, a more general audience, who will be intrigued by those characters but, unable to identify them with any certainty, will make their own identifications. Sonnets are thus private and public, pointedly addressed to particular individuals, pointedly failing to identify those individuals for those 'outsiders' who are condemned to 'groping in the darkness of biographical speculation' (2004: 235). Imagination prompts readers to speculation, but imagination also fills in the gaps where no biographical certainty is to be found.

Greenblatt, as I have already suggested, is happy to indulge in such speculation, because there is little else to fall back on when the records fail to offer up firm information. Indeed, his connection of Shakespeare and Southampton gives us some clear examples of this being enacted. Here is Greenblatt's description of how the two men may have met, despite their dramatically different social status. Southampton frequently went to the theatre, and thus:

> On *one of* these occasions, struck by Shakespeare's acting in a play *or* by his gifts as a writer *or* by his lively good looks, Southampton *could* easily have gone backstage after the performance to make his acquaintance, *or* asked *a mutual acquaintance* to introduce them, *or* simply and imperiously summoned him to a rendezvous.
>
> (2004: 228, my emphases)

Pinning down the likely date of their first encounter, if there was one, to 1591 or 1592, Greenblatt is forced to speculate about everything else. Look at the language of this quotation. 'On one of these occasions': no specific date is attainable. Perhaps Shakespeare's acting drew the

Earl to him. Or maybe it was the quality of his writing. Or his looks. Perhaps then Southampton went backstage. Or had a mutual friend, but we don't know who, introduce them. Or maybe he just summoned him. An ungenerous reading of this passage would suggest that it reveals little more than a series of gaps in this tale of their 'encounter' – when it occurred, what occurred, who was involved, where it took place, how it was achieved – but this would be to miss the point of Greenblatt's style in this book. He knows that this is all decidedly shaky, but he also knows that this is the best we are going to get, and that there is nothing to be gained by hiding this fact behind bold assertions or by choosing between options that must remain open.

There are limits to this imaginative process in the writing of biography, however, and at a key moment in this chapter, Greenblatt insists:

> Biographers have often succumbed to the temptation to turn these intimations of events into a full-blown romantic plot, but to do so requires pulling against the strong gravitational force of the individual poems. Shakespeare, who had an effortless genius at narrative, made certain that his sonnets would not yield an entirely coherent story.

> (2004: 247)

The gaps in the narrative of the sonnets open the space for meaning to be inserted – through imagination – just as the gaps in our knowledge of Shakespeare's life provoke us in similar ways. But we have to be careful what we wish for in filling these gaps. As one editor of the sonnets, Stephen Booth, wittily remarks: 'William Shakespeare was almost certainly homosexual, bisexual, or heterosexual. The sonnets provide no evidence on the matter' (Booth 2000: 548). That 'almost certainly' is fabulous. Similarly, Greenblatt's acts of imagination are a form of critical or narrative honesty, but they are also a way of generating narrative from the spaces left in the archive, from the holes in the whole.

Imagination, then, whether we are thinking about the relation between life and art or about the imaginative resources that lie behind a concept such as Purgatory, works in a dialectical manner. The world gives us experiences that have to be understood, and that prompt our desire to know. But these experiences also provoke us into thinking about another world, an other world, that is different, better or simply unfamiliar. These other worlds are constructed, poetic acts of the imagination, but the images that we use in thinking also make us behave in certain ways, even to the point of physical responses such as laughter, illness or death. Imagination draws upon the world for its content, but it also shapes our understanding of that content, guiding our response. Imagination is thus reproductive and productive, shadowing the real and casting a shadow that falls across the real. Imagination has a history, but history, to some extent, is always imagined.

SUMMARY

In Greenblatt's most recent books, he has developed his use of the idea of imagination. The history of the concept has led to imagination being seen as a bridge between sensation and reason, but it has also developed into a powerful force that shapes lives. In *Hamlet in Purgatory*, Purgatory is shown to be poetic, and Shakespeare's theatre draws on this poetic aspect, most obviously in the treatment of the ghost in *Hamlet*. Theatre thus takes on the intensity of a religious imagination. In writing about the life of Shakespeare in *Will in the World*, Greenblatt stresses the need for the biographer to employ imagination in trying to understand Shakespeare's imagination, but also shows the ways in which Shakespeare's own texts – especially the sonnets – invite the reader to use imagination to fill in the gaps in their narrative. Imagination is thus reproductive – representing the world and its objects – and productive, bringing into being a world that does not, and could not, exist in 'reality'.

AFTER GREENBLATT

It is only fitting to begin this final chapter with an anecdote. In 1997, there was a conference organized at the University of London, at which Stephen Greenblatt, Catherine Gallagher and others gathered under the heading 'After the New Historicism'. Very early on in the conference, after only one or two papers had been given, someone from the floor suggested that 'After the New Historicism' had to be understood, in the context of this conference at least, in the way that in art history paintings are described as 'After Holbein' or 'After Rembrandt'. That is to say, 'after' in this respect means that there is a certain degree of similarity between Greenblatt's work and that of others who follow him, their work is in imitation of his, or at least in the same style. What happens if we read the phrase 'After Greenblatt' in this way?

It would be very easy for me to list the critics and their works which have been, explicitly or implicitly, associated with Greenblatt and the new historicism. As Steven Mullaney puts it, in an essay entitled 'After the New Historicism':

> Like any genuinely seminal work, Greenblatt's has introduced new topics and parameters for subsequent analysis, new terms for debate and discussion. Greenblatt's critics ... sometimes fail to acknowledge the degree to which their differences depend, for their very articulation, upon the transformation of the field that Greenblatt (and others) made possible.
>
> (Mullaney in Hawkes 1996: 28)

In the section on Further reading (see p. 129 ff.) I have offered a few of the most notable instances, from a potential list that could go on for pages at least. It would not be an overstatement to say that new historicism has become the most influential movement within literary studies of the last twenty years. Part of the reason for this is explained by the institutional place of historicism (old and new), an influence that has only been accelerated and broadened by the appearance of anthologies used in teaching which are organized according to a new historicist paradigm. The most obvious of these are the widely used *Norton Anthology of English Literature* and the *Norton Shakespeare*. These works are, of course, edited by Stephen Greenblatt.

In the lengthy General Introduction by Greenblatt to the *Norton Shakespeare*, readers are first invited to consider the 'universal' aspects of Shakespeare's appeal through the ages, but by the end of the first section there is a crucial switch:

> An art virtually without end or limit but with an identifiable, localized, historical origin: Shakespeare's achievement defies the facile opposition between transcendent and time-bound. It is not necessary to choose between an account of Shakespeare as the scion of a particular culture and an account of him as a universal genius who created works that continually renew themselves across national and generational boundaries. On the contrary, crucial clues to understanding his art's remarkable power to soar beyond its originary time and place lie in the very soil from which that art sprang.
>
> (1997: 2)

There then follow over seventy pages on Shakespeare's world and the conditions of playing and printing in the early modern period. Having read the chapters on Greenblatt's key ideas in this book, you will no doubt recognize the significance of many of the terms in this quotation, most obviously in the references to crossing boundaries, to the soil from which art springs, and to the preference for that soil over ideas of individual genius. Whether Greenblatt wrote the Preface to the Eighth Edition of the *Norton Anthology of English Literature* is not certain (since it is not signed), but a clue may be found in its opening sentence: 'The outpouring of English literature overflows all boundaries . . .' (2006: page number varies by volume). In the next paragraph, readers will find that 'the boundaries between the literary and whatever is thought to be "nonliterary" are constantly challenged and redrawn'.

The argument is unmistakeable as an instance of new historicist practice in action, whether flowing directly from Greenblatt or not.

While this seems to be an obvious route for Greenblatt's ideas to exert an influence over students who are taught through these anthologies, nonetheless trying to gauge the extent of Greenblatt's influence over other critics is made more complicated by the lack of a systematic methodological programme for new historicism. As Gallagher and Greenblatt note, not without a certain comic self-parody:

> When years ago we first noticed in the annual job listing of the Modern Language Association that an English department was advertising for a specialist in new historicism, our response was incredulity. How could something that didn't really exist, that was only a few words gesturing toward a new interpretative practice, have become a 'field'? When did it happen and how could we not have noticed? If this was indeed a field, who could claim expertise in it and in what would such expertise exist? Surely, we of all people should know something of the history and the principles of new historicism, but what we knew above all was that it (or perhaps we) resisted systematization.
> (2000: 1–2)

Any attempt to follow Greenblatt must encounter this resistance. It is also the case that because Greenblatt's work itself draws from so many sources within so many disciplines, he tends not to invent a new terminology in the way that some thinkers do, and when others use terms similar to his own it is not always obvious whether they have taken them from him or from the sources in which he found them. The marks of the influence of someone such as, say, Jacques Derrida are often immediately apparent when a critic uses terms such as 'supplement', 'differance', 'pharmakon', 'hymen', and so on, because of the very specific sense that Derrida gives to these terms. By contrast, Greenblatt is less easy to track, although phrases such as 'self-fashioning', 'social energy', and 'cultural poetics' stand out. Greenblatt's influence is more readily to be seen in *what* critics analyse, as well as in the conjunctions that are made between literary and non-literary materials, in the use of anecdotes, and in the privileging of those elements of cultural production that fail to cohere into a system or world-picture in order to recast the narratives of a period and its culture.

One of the other problems that I have discovered in trying to write this section of this book – and indeed the book as a whole – is the result of a historical fact. Stephen Greenblatt is still alive. As such, any sense of what comes *after* Greenblatt will happily have to be suspended. But I also think that it will forever remain suspended, since it is impossible – and will remain impossible – to predict what might be made of his work by future generations. Just as Greenblatt is keenly aware of the ways in which Shakespeare's work continually renews itself as it is brought into relation with new contexts and practices, so his own work must similarly be open to such transformations, and these cannot be fully programmed and predicted by him, or me, or you.

There is, of course, another way of thinking about this idea of 'After Greenblatt', and it also stems from this notion of not knowing quite what Greenblatt's work will turn out to have been. That is, talking of being 'after' Greenblatt may be taken as an implication that some people are still struggling to work out what to do with his work, they are after him, seeking him out, as the police might be said to be after a criminal. To be after someone in this sense is to want something from that person, to want to do something to them or with them. Because Greenblatt's work has largely been concerned with Shakespeare and early modern culture, in the remainder of this chapter I will sketch out some of the ways in which critics have tried to 'get hold of' Greenblatt, either to understand his work by offering a critique of it, or else by trying to discover the paths by which his work might be led into new areas and in other directions. In each case, those who come after Greenblatt both do and do not imitate him. His insistence on attending to the particularity and contingency of a text or cultural artefact means that any attempt simply to 'do what Greenblatt would do' to it would have missed the whole point of Greenblatt's work. In this sense, Greenblatt *should* have no followers.

ALWAYS HISTORICIZE OR ONLY HISTORICIZE?

What has happened to new historicism? Linda Charnes, in a book which both follows and resists new historicism, notes pointedly that: 'Too many scholars of Renaissance culture read, in the important injunction "always historicize," an injunction to *only* historicize' (1995: 15). Charnes argues instead for a 'new hystericism', and the phrase marks her proximity and distance from new historicist practice, echoing but displacing it. This displacement comes in Charnes's work from a combination of some new historicist practices with other forms of theoretical inquiry to which new historicism has tended to be fairly resistant, including psychoanalysis and deconstruction. The mark of this in Greenblatt's work might be seen in his handling in *Hamlet in Purgatory* of books by Jacques Derrida (1994) and Marjorie Garber (1987), both of which deal with *Hamlet*, ghosts and materiality. Though both books would seem to merit a fuller discussion, they are given only a brief mention in footnotes (Greenblatt 2001: 297, nn. 16 and 17). Similarly, Jonathan Goldberg gloomily proposes that:

> the demise of 'theory' – or, better, the demise of its promise, especially in early modern studies – has prompted moves 'after theory', which is also to say, before theory. New historicism, insofar as it is still practiced, is virtually indistinguishable from old historicism.

(2003: x)

Goldberg's use of the phrase 'after theory' is instructive in understanding what 'After Greenblatt' might mean. What both Charnes and Goldberg note is a falling away from the idea of a historicism that was informed by theory. Echoing Goldberg, it is possible to think of many of those who have come *after* Greenblatt as actually coming *before* Greenblatt, so that in their attempts to historicize (but perhaps *only* to historicize), they have returned to a position that has lost precisely what was 'new' about the new historicism.

It would not be difficult to cite examples of this retreat into an apparently pre-theoretical state, before the Fall into theory. The engagement with theory, particularly the work of Foucault, in new historicism has remained one of the main points of objection to it. As Brian Vickers claims, in a characteristically sweeping attack on what he calls Current Literary Theory, all theory-driven readings are anachronistic, and 'anachronism distorts the past to suit the whims of the present' (2002: 541). This implies, of course, that Vickers has an undistorted and unmediated view of the past that allows him to judge the distortions of others. But equally there are those who think that new historicism isn't theoretical enough. Tom Cohen, for example, suggests that 'It is fairly easy, today, to see new historicism as itself a Reaganite phenomenon, with its reclamation of the semantic reserves of reference and its speculative mimeticism' (1994: 2). The deployment of certain critical tools is not only critically conservative, it also accords with a political conservatism, and in this comment Cohen is trying (however briefly) to historicize the new historicism. There is something impure about new historicism: for those committed to poststructuralism and deconstruction, it is too historicist; for those who prefer their history without theoretical underpinnings, it is not sufficiently historicist. In the next couple of pages, I will quickly outline some of the ways in which critics have responded to this impurity.

NEW MATERIALISM

One of the most distinctive aspects of new historicist practice has been a return to the archive. In the extension of the categories of literature to encompass non-literary and anecdotal materials, such an attention to archival sources has seen a proliferation of texts that are brought together with canonical literary texts. This has been coupled with the idea of cultural production as a material practice to produce what has come to be known as a 'new materialism', a critical mode that has also been described as a 'new new historicism'.

To take a single example for now, David Kastan's *Shakespeare and the Book* proceeds from the suggestion that:

A poem read as it was written by its author in ink on a sheet of foolscap is not identical with the 'same' poem read as printed in the Complete Works of the poet, or as published in the Norton anthology, or even as it is read online. Not only is it likely that the so-called accidentals of the texts will vary (if not some things more obviously substantive), but also that the modes and matrices of presentation themselves inevitably become part of the poem's structures of meaning, part, that is, of what determines how it is understood and valued.

(2001: 2–3)

It is not just that texts in different physical forms will look different – and by 'accidentals' Kastan means mistakes in spelling, typographical errors, and so on, which do not directly indicate a different meaning – but there will also be a different meaning attached to a text because it is a manuscript rather than a book, for example, or that derives from the way it is presented. As de Grazia (2001) puts it, in reading early modern material it is necessary to look *at* texts as well as to see *through* them. Kastan himself jokes that this materialist approach – characterized as it is by an analysis of objects rather than subjects within early modern culture – necessitates an attention to what are frequently none-too-exciting archival materials, and that it might be better named the 'new boredom'. What is emphasized in this work, however, is the fact that texts circulate not in ideal forms that communicate the author's intention but as physical, material commodities that have specific properties. As in Greenblatt's work, the book is seen to be a 'technology', and is related to other forms of cultural production at a particular moment in time and space.

For Kastan, this turn to the material production of the book is part of a wider project to read Shakespeare 'historically'. Kastan wishes to 'restore Shakespeare's artistry to the earliest conditions of its realisation', that is, to 'restore his works to the specific imaginative and material circumstances in which they were written and engaged' (1999: 15–17). Stressing the conditions of the production and reception of Shakespeare's works, Kastan wishes to oppose himself to theoretical readings of early modern culture, and sees in particular the idea of the 'situatedness' of the critic – in which the critic makes explicit his or her own position in the world, as Greenblatt frequently does – as a point of divergence between his own work and that of the new historicists.

This new materialism has little in common with cultural materialism, primarily because the concept of materiality that seems to underpin it is far removed from its roots in Marxist thought, and is really used to talk about objects and supposedly objective facts. In this sense, it concerns itself with the 'everyday' life of objects rather than providing a theoretical explanation of the relationship between those objects and the forms of social organization in which they are produced, consumed and exchanged. See Bruster 2003: 191–205; de Grazia *et al.* 1996; Harris 2000.

PRESENTISM

As I have shown in the earlier chapters in this book, Greenblatt's work – for all its insistence on the conditions in which a text originates and the connections and negotiations between the text and its various contexts – from time to time includes more explicit comments about contemporary culture (as in 'Resonance and Wonder', say). In this, his work is the kind to which Kastan objects. Much work within new historicism has been considerably less aware of the moment at which a critic produces her or his reading, however, and this has led to the emergence of what has been labelled 'presentism'. Deriving more from cultural materialism than from new historicism, and characterized by a commitment to addressing present political and cultural concerns, presentist critics explicitly distance themselves from the views expressed by Kastan on reading historically. Viewing the recovery of an authentic vision of the past as impossible (and noting Kastan's use of the word 'restore' to mark his sense that this might be possible), Terence Hawkes proposes that one problem lies in the appeal to facts about the past conditions of production and reception of literary texts. As Hawkes says, facts do not speak for themselves, and neither do texts. It is always the critic who selects the facts and selects the texts, and who puts them to some use. As such, there is no direct, unmediated access to the past that is not to some extent shaped by the concerns of whoever is investigating that past. Better then, says Hawkes, to make explicit the perspective that shapes such investigations. Here, however, emerges a different emphasis to Greenblatt's work. As Hawkes slyly remarks, a Shakespeare criticism that takes account of the impact of the present on critical discourse about the past 'will not yearn to speak with the dead. It will aim, in the end, to talk to the living' (Hawkes 2002: 1–4). For Hawkes, then, new historicism is not presentist enough, just as for Kastan, or for Jane Marcus, it is too presentist (see Marcus in Veeser 1989).

NEW AESTHETICISM

While Greenblatt always clearly communicates his love of literature, and the power that it has over him, some critics are troubled by the way in which he insists that art and literature are part of wider forms of cultural production. What seems to go missing in this emphasis on culture, some would argue, is a sense of art's specificity as an aesthetic phenomenon. In analysing the relationships between art and politics, ideology, society, subjectivity, and so on, it is seemingly easy to lose sight of the fact that art is art at all. In particular, there are strong philosophical reasons for trying to retain a space for art that is not simply cultural. Stemming from a debate in philosophy, and particularly the work of J. M. Bernstein and Andrew Bowie, this has been taken up by early modern and other critics as a way of rethinking some of the suppositions of new historicism. In their introduction to a collection of essays entitled *The New Aestheticism*, John Joughin and Simon Malpas propose that 'an adequate thinking of modernity requires an investigation of the aesthetic and, reciprocally, the discussion of the impact of art and literature on contemporary culture needs a way of situating this culture in relation to the history of modern politics and philosophy' (Joughin and Malpas 2003: 9). This is significant because if critics wish to think through any idea of the early modern, then this obviously has to bear some relationship to the definition of modernity (for discussions of early modern literature in this book, see the essays by Dollimore, Joughin, and Robson). Interestingly, Greenblatt delivered a paper at the 2005 meeting of the Shakespeare Association of America in a plenary session entitled 'The Mark of Beauty', and so it seems that his work in the near future will engage explicitly with aesthetic questions.

DOES NEW HISTORICISM HAVE A FUTURE?

The new historicism has been pronounced dead on more than one occasion. But there is something profoundly historicist about such pronouncements, since they imply that ideas and modes of thinking are the product of, and are contained by, a specific cultural moment. New historicism itself gives us reasons to think that this is inadequate. Yet the impression that new historicism has passed its 'use by' date persists. As Douglas Bruster puts it, however, 'New historicism can be seen as a thing of the past precisely because so many of its assumptions and practices have become standard and hence less visible to us' (Bruster 2003: 29). Whether or not people call themselves new historicists, and whether or not they make use of terms such as self-fashioning or social energy, the influence of Greenblatt's work seems too firmly embedded in literary studies as it is currently constituted for claims that new historicism is dead or finished with to be treated with too much seriousness.

FURTHER READING

This annotated bibliography will be divided into three sections. First, there is a section which details the major works by Greenblatt, including articles not included in his books. Second, I identify some new historicist works, anthologies, and collections by or featuring Greenblatt and other writers. Third, I suggest some critical discussions of Greenblatt and new historicism that are most appropriate for student readers.

WORKS BY STEPHEN GREENBLATT

—— (1973) *Sir Walter Ralegh: The Renaissance Man and His Roles*, New Haven, CT: Yale University Press.

In some senses a precursor to *Renaissance Self-Fashioning*, this book (based on Greenblatt's doctoral thesis) analyses the prominent Elizabethan courtier, Sir Walter Raleigh, seeking to explore the ways in which Raleigh attempted to 'fashion his own identity as a work of art'. Greenblatt focuses on the contradictions within Raleigh's life, his complex relation to the world he inhabited, and the inadequacy of the distinction between life and art in thinking about Raleigh's life. Ideas such as role-playing and theatricality are central to the argument, leading to a sense that Raleigh's project is achieved when he ascends the scaffold for his final performance at his execution.

—— (1980) *Renaissance Self-Fashioning: From More to Shakespeare*, Chicago, IL: University of Chicago Press.

This is the book that launched Greenblatt's reputation, and is often taken as a starting point for the dominance of new historicism in renaissance literary studies. In a series of deft and dense readings of canonical texts by Thomas More, William Tyndale, Thomas Wyatt, Edmund Spenser, Christopher Marlowe and William Shakespeare, Greenblatt lays out his influential notion of 'self-fashioning'. Because of its range and length, this remains the best place to start a serious engagement with his work, and in many ways is still his most important book.

—— (1988) *Shakespearean Negotiations: The Circulation of Social Energy in Renaissance England*, Oxford: Clarendon Press.

Shakespearean Negotiations is, perhaps, the book that has aroused the most controversy in Greenblatt's *oeuvre*. Its most famous chapter 'Invisible Bullets', appearing in several anthologies, contains the crucial argument on subversion and containment that raised, and continues to raise, the political dimension of new historicist practice in a clear manner. The book's central concept of 'social energy' not only allows Greenblatt to open up readings of Shakespearean texts alongside non-literary material, providing a rationale for what might otherwise appear to be rather arbitrary connections, it also prompts a consideration of the role that Shakespeare and his texts continue to exert beyond the early modern period.

—— (1990) *Learning to Curse: Essays in Early Modern Culture*, London and New York: Routledge.

This collection brings together essays published between 1976 and 1990. It includes some of Greenblatt's most important statements on methodology, including his attempts to outline his notion of cultural poetics, and to relate this poetics to other critical modes, such as psychoanalysis and anthropology. Topics covered by the essays include Shakespeare, Marlowe, colonialism, and anti-Semitism. Of particular interest are 'Psychoanalysis and Renaissance Culture', 'Towards a Poetics of Culture' and 'Resonance and Wonder'. This collection acts as a useful primer for the work which established the new historicism, although it has perhaps now been supplanted by *The Greenblatt Reader* (see p. 132).

—— (1991) *Marvelous Possessions: The Wonder of the New World*, Oxford: Clarendon Press.

Taking on his Jewish inheritance more explicitly than in most of his other work, this book addresses competing early modern discourses on Jerusalem and its religious and political dimensions. Based on a series of lectures, this is a highly readable book. It engages particularly with the travel narratives produced by writers such as Mandeville and Columbus, detailing the encounters between European travellers and the inhabitants of the New World. It is particularly important for rethinking ideas of mimesis, and in its elaboration of wonder.

—— (1997) 'What is the History of Literature?', *Critical Inquiry* 23, 460–81.

Trying to answer the question in his title, Greenblatt makes some valuable observations on the relation between 'literature' and 'literacy', looking at both in terms of specific historical understandings of them as categories. These are, in turn, related to the question of teaching literature in the modern academy, and he comments on Bacon, Shakespeare and the American university through a concern for the ways in which literature and literacy have been involved in the definition and redefinition of social status. Contains some interesting anecdotes about his early career and Jewish identity.

—— (2000) *Practicing New Historicism* (with Catherine Gallagher), Chicago, IL: University of Chicago Press.

This co-written book offers the clearest explanation of the influences and concerns that motivated new historicism, as well as providing chapters that exemplify it as a practice. While the authors claim joint responsibility for the book, three chapters (1, 3 and 5) are best thought of as being by Greenblatt, not least because 1 and 5 were initially published in article form under his name alone. Notably, the most prominent source for their practice is identified as the German romantic philosopher Johann Gottfried von Herder, and the volume opens up new questions concerning the relationship between new historicism and aesthetics.

—— (2001) *Hamlet in Purgatory*, Princeton, NJ: Princeton University Press.

Traces the roots of Shakespeare's *Hamlet* in the medieval and early modern practices of mourning and burial, emphasizing the changing attitudes towards Purgatory. There is some fascinating material on ghosts, possession, imagination and questions of belief and believability. By no means the most accessible of Greenblatt's works, especially in the earlier chapters, it nevertheless offers an intriguing and original route into thinking about a play that has received a stupefying level of commentary.

—— (2004) *Will in the World: How Shakespeare Became Shakespeare*, London: Jonathan Cape.

A somewhat surprising turn in Greenblatt's career, perhaps, in that this is, in many respects, a conventional biography. More plausibly, it fits with the suggestions that Greenblatt made when President of the Modern Language Association that academic critics should make attempts to reach a broader non-academic audience. This highly readable book is notable among Shakespeare biographies, however, for its insistence on the necessary role of imagination in life-writing.

—— (2005) *The Greenblatt Reader*, ed. Michael Payne, Oxford: Blackwell.

This collection of essays is the best place for someone new to Greenblatt's work to begin. It offers an opportunity to see the range of his work, including both chapters from his most well-known books and previously uncollected essays, arranged in four sections and covering culture and new historicism, Renaissance studies, his work on Shakespeare, and more disparate occasional pieces. The volume also includes a brief introduction by the editor and a useful (although not entirely accurate) bibliography (1965–2003).

NEW HISTORICISM AND CULTURAL MATERIALISM

Dollimore, Jonathan (2004) *Radical Tragedy: Religion, Ideology and Power in the Drama of Shakespeare and his Contemporaries*, 3rd edn, Basingstoke: Palgrave Macmillan.

One of the foremost works of cultural materialism, first appearing in 1984. Dollimore begins by establishing and challenging many of the conventional ways of reading and thinking about tragedy, before proceeding to readings of plays by Marston, Marlowe, Jonson, Shakespeare, Webster and others. The second and third editions of the book are especially useful in laying out some of the history of the book's writing and reception, and as such the three volumes chart the fortunes of cultural materialism. In the introduction to the third edition, Dollimore re-evaluates his own original project, as well as relating it to subsequent events, including September 11.

Dollimore, Jonathan and Alan Sinfield (eds) (1994) *Political Shakespeare: Essays in Cultural Materialism*, 2nd edn, Manchester: Manchester University Press.

In what remains the best place to begin to think about cultural materialism, the essays collected here act both as examples of cultural materialist practice and as manifestos for the project as a whole. The first edition appeared in 1985, and contained what became classic essays by Dollimore, Sinfield, Greenblatt, Brown, McLuskie and others, including an Afterword by Raymond Williams. The second edition adds further essays by Dollimore and Sinfield. Dollimore's introduction is especially helpful, discussing both cultural materialism and new historicism.

Drakakis, John (ed.) (1985) *Alternative Shakespeares*, London: Methuen.

Like *Political Shakespeare*, this collection of essays had a profound impact on Shakespeare studies and on early modern studies more generally. This volume is less focused on cultural materialism than its counterpart, and includes essays that are more overtly influenced by deconstruction, psychoanalysis and poststructuralist feminism, but it retains the sense of attempting to present alternatives to the then-dominant ways of reading Shakespeare. Contains influential essays by Hawkes, Rose, Belsey, Barker and Hulme, and Dollimore and Sinfield.

Greenblatt, Stephen (ed.) (1988) *Representing the English Renaissance*, Berkeley, CA: University of California Press.

As Greenblatt notes in his introduction to this collection on sixteenth- and seventeenth-century topics, what unites these essays is first of all the fact that they were all originally published in the journal *Representations*, and second that they are all concerned with what he calls 'the domain of art', in which definitions of the literary are not taken for granted. The essays diverge in some respects, but there is a sense of shared interests. Includes essays by Greenblatt, Fineman, Montrose, Mullaney, Orgel and others associated with new historicism.

Montrose, Louis (1996) *The Purpose of Playing: Shakespeare and the Cultural Politics of the Elizabethan Theater*, Chicago, IL: University of Chicago Press.

An analysis of the politics of representation, and especially the place of the professional theatre in the Elizabethan period. Focused on Shakespeare's *A Midsummer Night's Dream*, Montrose stresses the workings of ideology in cultural production. The book also includes some consideration of the methodology of new historicism.

Ryan, Kiernan (ed.) (1996) *New Historicism and Cultural Materialism: A Reader*, London: Arnold.

A useful anthology for beginners, which begins with brief extracts labelled as sources for new historicism and cultural materialism, including work by Geertz, Foucault, Althusser, Williams, Derrida and Benjamin. The second section includes essays by Gallagher, Greenblatt, Sinfield, Belsey, and others, that offer some methodological discussion, and the third gives examples of readings of different periods in literary history. Ryan's brief introduction raises some important issues.

Veeser, H. Aram (ed.) (1989) *The New Historicism*, London and New York: Routledge.

A solid collection, valuable largely for its combination of essays by the central practitioners of new historicism – including Greenblatt, Gallagher, Montrose and Fineman – and material more sceptical and occasionally overtly hostile to it. Useful in tracing both the foundations of new historicism and the early response to it. See especially the essays by Lentricchia, Graff, Newton, Marcus and Pecora.

—— (1994) *The New Historicism Reader*, London and New York: Routledge.

Similar to the earlier volume edited by Veeser, this also attempts to survey the new historicist field, again including some of the opposition, but this time gives examples of new historicism rather than responses to it. Essays by Greenblatt, Orgel, Gallagher, Fineman and Montrose are present, and there is a helpful bibliography that outlines both new historicist work and discussions of it.

Wilson, Richard and Richard Dutton (eds) (1992) *New Historicism and Renaissance Drama*, Hemel Hempstead: Harvester Wheatsheaf.

A useful collection of essays, including two pieces by Greenblatt ('Marlowe and the Will to Absolute Play' and 'Invisible Bullets') and

others by Barker, Belsey, Dollimore, Montrose, Tennenhouse, *et al.*
Includes Jean Howard's article 'The New Historicism in Renaissance
Studies', a helpful introduction by Richard Wilson, and a thoughtful
postscript by Richard Dutton on some of the objections to new
historicism and cultural materialism.

WORKS ON AND AROUND GREENBLATT

Bradshaw, Graham (1993) *Misrepresentations: Shakespeare and the
Materialists*, Ithaca, NY: Cornell University Press.
   A spirited and detailed attempt to disentangle Shakespeare's plays
from the readings provided by new historicist and cultural materialist
critics which argues, as the title suggests, that the plays are diminished
by those readings. Despite this opposition to Greenblatt's work in particular, Bradshaw wishes to retain the idea of a poetics of culture.

Brannigan, John (1998) *New Historicism and Cultural Materialism*,
Basingstoke: Macmillan.
   A valuable introductory text, combining some general descriptions
of historicism in the first section with case studies of particular texts
in the second, including Conrad, Gilman, Tennyson and Yeats.

Bruster, Douglas (2003) *Shakespeare and the Question of Culture: Early
Modern Literature and the Cultural Turn*, Basingstoke and New York:
Palgrave Macmillan.
   An excellent though not always easy book that traces the uses of
culture as a concept in contemporary criticism, with some pithy analysis
of new historicist work as well as some intriguing suggestions for how
that work might progress. Very good on the forms that argumentation
takes, and should take, as well as what counts as good evidence. Highly
recommended, though not necessarily for beginners.

Colebrook, Clare (1997) *New Literary Histories: New Historicism and
Contemporary Criticism*, Manchester and New York: Manchester University
Press.
   The title is a little misleading, as this is actually a much more ambitious
book than it might appear to be. Contains chapters on Greenblatt and
new historicism and Williams and cultural materialism, but also discusses
Foucault, Bourdieu, de Certeau, Althusser and others. As such, new
historicism is very much placed in a context of critical thinking to
which it is connected and from which it is distinguished.

Felperin, Howard (1992) *The Uses of the Canon: Elizabethan Literature and Contemporary Theory*, Oxford: Clarendon Press.

Included here because of an essay on cultural poetics and cultural materialism, this book is profoundly indebted to deconstruction in providing readings of early modern texts. The essay on historicisms surveys much of the negative material and provides a sceptical commentary of its own on the problems of new historicism in relation to a philosophy of history.

Grady, Hugh (1994) *The Modernist Shakespeare: Critical Texts in a Material World*, Oxford: Clarendon Press.

This book only includes a brief discussion of new historicism directly, but it charts the different strands in twentieth-century Shakespeare criticism in ways that are extremely useful for working out where the new historicism fits. Grady is much closer to cultural materialism, and has been central to the recent movement in favour of 'presentism'.

Halpern, Richard (1997) *Shakespeare Among the Moderns*, Ithaca, NY: Cornell University Press.

The opening chapter, 'Shakespeare in the Tropics: From High Modernism to New Historicism', includes discussion of Greenblatt, relating his work to that of modernist critics such as T. S. Eliot, and emphasizing the continuities between a modernist reading of Shakespeare that 'displaced' his work in terms of their canonical place in English literature, and a new historicist practice that displaces Shakespeare by reading his texts against non-European cultural others.

Hamilton, Paul (1996) *Historicism*, London and New York: Routledge.

Includes new historicism in a survey that extends from the ancient Greeks to the present. Wonderful in many respects, this is a book that is challenging even for those who know their way around the field, and is not recommended for novices. But there is much of interest here, and Hamilton's conception of historicism is rigorous but also wide-ranging, including discussion of Freud, Derrida, postcolonialism, postmodernism and feminisms.

Kelly, Philippa (ed.) (2002) *The Touch of the Real: Essays in Early Modern Culture*, Crawley: University of Western Australia Press.

Collection of essays published in honour of Greenblatt, containing material by Australian scholars. It includes Greenblatt's 'Racial Memory and Literary History', an essay that touches on Shakespeare, Jane Austen, and others, and includes some autobiographical anecdotes about his Lithuanian grandparents.

Pechter, Edward (1995) *What Was Shakespeare? Renaissance Plays and Changing Critical Practice*, Ithaca, NY: Cornell University Press.

In this survey of Shakespeare criticism from the 1960s onwards, Pechter includes a chapter on Greenblatt and new historicism that is sceptical of the politics of new historicism while also admitting the positive effects that this work has had in allowing for new ways of thinking and writing about Shakespeare.

Pieters, Jurgen (2001) *Moments of Negotiation: The New Historicism of Stephen Greenblatt*, Amsterdam: Amsterdam University Press.

The first book-length study of Greenblatt's work, *Moments of Negotiation* offers a sense of the theoretical background to Greenblatt's work as well as detailed treatments of his work and those texts that he analyses. Contains many surveys of other critics, but in part the range attempted – while laudable in itself – means that the discussion is not always entirely convincing.

Pieters, Jurgen (ed.) (1999) *Critical Self-Fashioning: Stephen Greenblatt and the New Historicism*, New York: Peter Lang.

Collection of essays largely by European critics, thus providing an interesting counterpoint to the largely British and American reception of new historicism that dominates. Also includes valuable essays by Jonathan Gil Harris and David Schalkwyk.

Porter, Carolyn (1990) 'Are we being historical yet?', in *The States of Theory: History, Art, and Critical Discourse*, ed. David Carroll, Stanford, CA: Stanford University Press, 27–62.

Influential and incisive essay that focuses on the politics of new historicism, arguing in favour of cultural materialism, and especially the work of Raymond Williams. Argues that historicization always implies some political position, but that criticism at the time she was writing had not yet succeeded in being genuinely historical.

Strier, Richard (1995) *Resistant Structures: Particularity, Radicalism, and Renaissance Texts*, Berkeley, CA: University of California Press.

Published in Greenblatt's 'The New Historicism: Studies in Cultural Poetics' series, this book is nonetheless sceptical of some of the claims and consequences of Greenblatt's work, most obviously in chapter 4 'The New Historicism', which focuses on *Renaissance Self-Fashioning* and some of Greenblatt's essays.

Wilson, Scott (1995) *Cultural Materialism: Theory and Practice*, Oxford: Blackwell.

Includes a chapter on cultural materialism directly, and another on Greenblatt and new historicism. Much of the rest of the book is given over to challenging many of the assumptions of these movements, predominantly through the work of Georges Bataille. Again, not introductory, but always clear and provocative.

WORKS CITED

Adorno, Theodor W. (1991) *Notes to Literature*, vol. 1, trans. Shierry Weber Nicholsen, New York: Columbia University Press.

Anderson, Benedict (1991) *Imagined Communities: Reflections on the Origin and Spread of Nationalism*, rev. edn, London and New York: Verso.

Aristotle (1995) *Complete Works*, ed. Jonathan Barnes, 2 vols, Princeton, NJ: Princeton University Press.

Auerbach, Erich (1968) *Mimesis: The Representation of Reality in Western Literature*, trans. Willard R. Trask, Princeton, NJ: Princeton University Press.

Austin, J. L. (1976) *How to Do Things With Words*, Oxford: Oxford University Press.

Barthes, Roland (1989) *The Rustle of Language*, trans. Richard Howard, Berkeley, CA: University of California Press.

Benjamin, Walter (2002) *Selected Writings, vol. 3: 1935–1938*, eds Howard Eiland and Michael W. Jennings, Cambridge, MA: Belknap/ Harvard University Press.

—— (2003) *Selected Writings, vol. 4: 1938–1940*, eds Howard Eiland and Michael W. Jennings, Cambridge, MA: Belknap/Harvard University Press.

Booth, Stephen (ed.) (2000) *Shakespeare's Sonnets*, New Haven, CT and London: Yale University Press.

Bossy, John (1985) *Christianity in the West 1400–1700*, Oxford: Oxford University Press.

Bruster, Douglas (2003) *Shakespeare and the Question of Culture: Early Modern Literature and the Cultural Turn*, Basingstoke: Palgrave Macmillan.

Burke, Sean (1992) *The Death and Return of the Author: Criticism and Subjectivity in Barthes, Foucault and Derrida*, Edinburgh: Edinburgh University Press.

Caygill, Howard (1995) *A Kant Dictionary*, Oxford: Blackwell.

Charnes, Linda (1995) *Notorious Identity: Materializing the Subject in Shakespeare*, Cambridge, MA: Harvard University Press.

Cohen, Tom (1994) *Anti-Mimesis: From Plato to Hitchcock*, Cambridge: Cambridge University Press.

Culler, Jonathan (1997) *Literary Theory: A Very Short Introduction*, Oxford: Oxford University Press.

De Grazia, Margreta (2001) 'Shakespeare and the Craft of Language', in *The Cambridge Companion to Shakespeare*, eds Margreta De Grazia and Stanley Wells, Cambridge: Cambridge University Press, pp. 49–64.

——, Maureen Quilligan and Peter Stallybrass (eds) (1996) *Subject and Object in Renaissance Culture*, Cambridge: Cambridge University Press.

Derrida, Jacques (1994) *Specters of Marx: The State of the Debt, the Work of Mourning, and the New International*, trans. Peggy Kamuf, London and New York: Routledge.

Dollimore, Jonathan and Alan Sinfield (eds) (1994) *Political Shakespeare: Essays in Cultural Materialism*, 2nd edn, Manchester: Manchester University Press.

Duffy, Eamon (1992) *The Stripping of the Altars: Traditional Religion in England 1400–1580*, New Haven, CT and London: Yale University Press.

Fineman, Joel (1991) *The Subjectivity Effect in Western Literary Tradition: Essays Toward the Release of Shakespeare's Will*, Cambridge, MA: MIT Press.

Foucault, Michel (1990) *The History of Sexuality, Volume 1: An Introduction*, trans. Robert Hurley, Harmondsworth: Penguin.

—— (2002) *Power: Essential Works of Foucault 1954–1984, vol. 3*, ed. James D. Faubion, Harmondsworth: Penguin.

Freud, Sigmund (2003) *The Uncanny*, trans. David McLintock, Harmondsworth: Penguin.

Gallagher, C. and S. Greenblatt (2000) *Practicing New Historicism*, Chicago, IL: University of Chicago Press.

Garber, Marjorie (1987) *Shakespeare's Ghost Writers: Literature as Uncanny Causality*, London and New York: Routledge.

—— (2003) *Quotation Marks*, London and New York: Routledge.

Gebauer, Gunter and Christoph Wulf (1995) *Mimesis: Culture, Art, Society*, trans. Don Reneau, Berkeley, CA: University of California Press.

Geertz, Clifford (1993a) *The Interpretation of Cultures: Selected Essays*, London: Fontana. First published 1973.

—— (1993b) *Local Knowledge: Further Essays in Interpretive Anthroplogy*, London: Fontana. First published 1983.

—— (2001) *Available Light: Anthropological Reflections on Philosophical Topics*, Princeton, NJ: Princeton University Press. First published 2000.

Girard, René (1988) *'To Double Business Bound': Essays on Literature, Mimesis, and Anthropology*, London: Athlone.

Goldberg, Jonathan (2003) *Shakespeare's Hand*, Minneapolis, MN: University of Minnesota Press.

Grady, Hugh (1994) *The Modernist Shakespeare: Critical Texts in a Material World*, Oxford: Clarendon Press.

Greenblatt, Stephen (1973) *Sir Walter Ralegh: The Renaissance Man and His Roles*, New Haven, CT: Yale University Press.

—— (1980) *Renaissance Self-Fashioning: From More to Shakespeare*, Chicago, IL: University of Chicago Press.

—— (1982) *The Power of Forms in the English Renaissance*, Norman, OK: Pilgrim.

—— (ed.) (1988) *Representing the English Renaissance*, Berkeley, CA: University of California Press.

—— (1990) *Shakespearean Negotiations: The Circulation of Social Energy in Renaissance England*, Oxford: Clarendon Press. First published 1988.

—— (1991) *Marvelous Possessions: The Wonder of the New World*, Oxford: Clarendon Press.

—— (1992) *Learning to Curse: Essays in Early Modern Culture*, London: Routledge.

—— (1997) 'What is the History of Literature?', *Critical Inquiry* 23: 460–81.

—— (2001) *Hamlet in Purgatory*, Princeton, NJ: Princeton University Press.

—— (2004) *Will in the World: How Shakespeare Became Shakespeare*, London: Jonathan Cape.

—— (2005) *The Greenblatt Reader*, ed. Michael Payne, Oxford: Blackwell.

Greene, Thomas M. (1982) *The Light in Troy: Imitation and Discovery in Renaissance Poetry*, New Haven, CT: Yale University Press.

Haigh, Christopher (1993) *English Reformations: Religion, Politics, and Society under the Tudors*, Oxford: Oxford University Press.

Harris, Jonathan Gil (2000) 'The New New Historicism's *Wunderkammer* of Objects', *European Journal of English Studies* 4.3: 111–23.

Hawkes, Terence (2002) *Shakespeare in the Present*, London and New York: Routledge.

—— (ed.) (1996) *Alternative Shakespeares, vol. 2*, London and New York: Routledge.

Hegel, G. W. F. (1967) *The Phenomenology of Mind*, trans. J. B. Baillie, New York: Harper.

—— (1977) *Phenomenology of Spirit*, trans. A. V. Miller, Oxford: Oxford University Press.

—— (1998) *Aesthetics: Lectures on Fine Art*, trans. T. M. Knox, 2 vols, Oxford: Oxford University Press.

Herder, Johann Gottfried von (1997) *On World History: An Anthology*, eds Hans Adler and Ernest A. Menze, London: M. E. Sharpe.

—— (2002) *Philosophical Writings*, ed. Michael N. Forster, Cambridge: Cambridge University Press.

Herman, Peter C. (ed.) (2004) *Historicizing Theory*, Albany, NY: SUNY Press.

Jameson, Fredric (2002) *The Political Unconscious*, London: Routledge.

Joughin, John J. and Simon Malpas (eds) (2003) *The New Aestheticism*, Manchester: Manchester University Press.

Kant, Immanuel (1987) *Critique of Judgment*, trans. Werner S. Pluhar, Indianapolis, IN: Hackett.

Kastan, David Scott (1999) *Shakespeare After Theory*, London and New York: Routledge.

—— (2001) *Shakespeare and the Book*, Cambridge: Cambridge University Press.

Kearney, Richard (1988) *The Wake of Imagination*, London: Hutchinson.

Lever, J. W. (1971) *The Tragedy of State*, London: Methuen.

Marx, Karl (1992) 'The Eighteenth Brumaire of Louis Bonaparte', in *Surveys from Exile. Political Writings: Volume 2*, ed. David Fernbach, Harmondsworth: Penguin, pp. 143–249.

Melberg, Arne (1995) *Theories of Mimesis*, Cambridge: Cambridge University Press.

Montaigne, Michel de (1991) *The Complete Essays*, trans. M. A. Screech, Harmondsworth: Penguin.

Montrose, Louis (1986) 'Renaissance Literary Studies and the Subject of History', *English Literary Renaissance* 16: 5–12.

More, Thomas (1989) *Utopia*, eds George M. Logan and Robert M. Adams, Cambridge: Cambridge University Press.

Orgel, Stephen (1975) *The Illusion of Power: Political Theater in the English Renaissance*, Berkeley, CA: University of California Press.

Plato (1989) *Collected Dialogues of Plato, including the letters*, eds Edith Hamilton and Huntington Cairns, Princeton, NJ: Princeton University Press.

Royle, Nicholas (2003) *The Uncanny*, Manchester: Manchester University Press.

Sartre, Jean-Paul (1989) *Existentialism and Humanism*, London: Methuen.

Shelley, Percy Bysshe (2002) *Shelley's Poetry and Prose*, eds Donald H. Reiman and Neil Fraistrat, New York: W. W. Norton.

Veeser, H. Aram (ed.) (1989) *The New Historicism*, London and New York: Routledge.

Vickers, Brian (2002) *Shakespeare, Co-Author: A Historical Study of Five Collaborative Plays*, Oxford: Oxford University Press.

Williams, Raymond (1983) *Keywords: A Vocabulary of Culture and Society*, London: Flamingo.

—— (1989) *Marxism and Literature*, Oxford: Oxford University Press.

Young, Robert (1990) *White Mythologies: Writing History and the West*, London and New York: Routledge.

Žižek, Slavoj (1989) *The Sublime Object of Ideology*, London: Verso.

—— (ed.) (1994) *Mapping Ideology*, London: Verso.

INDEX